THIS   SPECIAL   COPY

IS PRESENTED TO YOU WITH OUR

SEASON'S GREETINGS

& BEST WISHES

FOR A HAPPY & PROSPEROUS

NEW YEAR

1 9 9 6

Blackwell North America, Inc.

LAKE OSWEGO, OREGON

BLACKWOOD, NEW JERSEY

NOW
ALL WE NEED
IS A TITLE

Also by André Bernard:

Rotten Rejections: A Literary Companion

Now all we need is a Title

Famous Book Titles and How They Got That Way

ANDRÉ BERNARD

W.W. Norton & Company
New York   London

Langston Hughes's "Harlem: A Dream Deferred"
© 1951 by Langston Hughes. Reproduced by
permission of Alfred A. Knopf.

"American Names" by Stephen Vincent Benet from *The Selected
Works of Stephen Vincent Benet.* Copyright 1927 by
Stephen Vincent Benet, copyright © renewed 1955 by
Rosemary Carr Benet. Reprinted by permission of
Brandt & Brandt, Literary Agents, Inc.

The text of this book is composed in Weiss 10/12
with the display set in Weiss Bold.
Composition and manufacturing by The Maple-Vail Book
Manufacturing Group.
Book design by Hudson Studio

Library of Congress Cataloging-in-Publication Data

Bernard, André, 1956–
Now all we need is a title : famous book titles and how they got
that way / by André Bernard.
000 p. 000cm.
1. Books and reading.   2. Titles of books.   I. Title.
       Z1003.B4926   1994
       028—dc20   94-18613

ISBN 0-393-03694-4

W. W. Norton & Company Ltd.
500 Fifth Avenue, New York, N.Y. 10110

W. W. Norton & Company, Ltd.
10 Coptic Street, London WC1A 1PU

3 4 5 6 7 8 9 0

INTRODUCTION

$\mathcal{A}$LTHOUGH I work in book publishing and handle manu-
scripts and books, phone calls from authors, catalogs
from publishers, and a remarkable amount of book-related
paperwork every day, I can't remember a book title to save
my life. One of my colleagues, who is equally over-
whelmed, can *only* remember titles; as the books cascade
over her desk, one after the other by the hundreds, the sum
total becomes a multi-paged blur, and only a catchy title
will single out a potential winner from the pile.

Authors face this dilemma with every new book they
write: Does the title really matter? "I have never been a title
man," groused John Steinbeck. "I don't give a damn what it
is called." (Despite his tough stance, this was quite untrue.
Steinbeck worked hard at his titles and the results are
among the most memorable in American literature.) Perhaps his attitude is shared by the public. I suspect, though,
that most readers would agree with Samuel Butler's senti-
ments on the subject: " 'The Ancient Mariner' would not
have taken so well if it had been called 'The Old Sailor.' "
East of Eden does catch one's attention, and so do *Gone with
the Wind* and *Tess of the d'Urbervilles* and *Bleak House*—they
mean something beyond their alluring sound, something
that *The Salinas Valley* or *Pansy* or *The Body and Soul of Sue* or
Tom-All-Alone's Factory that Got Into Chancery and Never Got Out
just don't.* There's no lesson to be drawn here, just a kind
of respectful puzzlement at the creative process.

---

* *These were early working titles for the above-named.*

The book you are reading is an anecdotal account of how some of the most well-known book and play titles came to be. It is not meant to be a comprehensive compendium of *every* catchy title, but rather a lighthearted look at a struggle that has bedeviled writers for centuries. And when you, the reader, come to write your own masterpiece, remember the trials, near-misses, and complete disasters of your colleagues in the naming game. As you will see, titles come about in the most curious ways.

A few thanks are in order. Among the writers who gave generously of their time to delve into their own experiences of title-hunting are Peter Benchley, Roy Blount, Jr., Helen Gurley Brown, Jim Charlton, Richard Condon, Evan Connell, Nelson DeMille, Gail Godwin, Sue Grafton, Bel Kaufman, John Nichols, M. Scott Peck, Charles Portis, Peter Schwed, Joseph Wambaugh, and Eudora Welty. I am grateful to them. Gerald Howard at W. W. Norton whipped a pile of paper into shape, and gave it a title as well, wisely discarding the lousy title I had come up with.* Jennie McGregor Bernard did the hardest work of all—she started the project and she finished it. And Julie Merberg came up with the idea in the first place.

Finally, this book is for my friend Ken McCormick, a great and durable editor who thought up some of this century's finest book titles.

André Bernard
1994

---

* *Untitled.*

NOW
ALL WE NEED
IS A TITLE

JAMES AGEE
Let Us Now Praise Famous Men (1941)

*T*HE thirty-one-year-old Agee, who reviewed books for *Time*, was devastated when his enormously moving collaboration with photographer Walker Evans, a study of poverty among laborers called *Three Tenant Families*, was rejected by its publisher as offensive and generally disorganized. Agee refused to change the content of his book. He did give it a new title, though, one that both evoked the tragedy of the people he wrote about and commemorated the three years he had spent writing something that, it seemed, was never to be published. He found his title in the Bible, in Ecclesiasticus (*not* Ecclesiastes): "Let us now praise famous men, and our fathers that begat us. . . . Their bodies were buried in peace; but their name liveth for evermore."

⁀

No sooner had I settled in my house and library than I undertook the composition of the first Volume of my history. At the outset all was dark and doubtful: even the title of the work, the true era of the decline and fall of the Empire, the limits of the Introduction, the division of the chapters, and the order of the narrative; and I was often tempted to cast away the labors of seven years . . .   EDWARD GIBBON

❧

EDWARD ALBEE
Who's Afraid of Virginia Woolf? (1962)

*O*NE of the most famous and enigmatic of all play titles found its name in a bar. In the 1950s would-be writer Albee liked to go for a drink to a well-patronized bar on Tenth Street in New York's Greenwich Village. On the ground floor there was a big mirror where people used to scrawl graffiti. One day Albee was in the bar drinking a beer and saw "Who's Afraid of Virginia Woolf?" written on the mirror in soap. It stuck with him, and when he began writing his play, which was set on a university campus, he was reminded of the odd message. " 'Who's afraid of Virginia Woolf,' " Albee once said, "means who's afraid of the big *bad* wolf . . . who's afraid of living without false illusions. And it did strike me as being a rather typical university, intellectual joke."

❧

NELSON ALGREN
The Man with the Golden Arm (1949)

*D*ESPITE a generally good relationship with Doubleday, his publisher, Chicago novelist Algren was quick to look for potential trouble from editors, and always suspected them of somehow wanting to hurt him. The enthusiasm of Doubleday's editor-in-chief, Ken McCormick, for the title *The Neon Wilderness* put him off. "The minute I liked it," McCormick recalled, "he hated it. So then I had to get a third party to convince him that he had a good title." Doubleday's endorsement of *The Man with the Golden Arm* for

Algren's tough account of the fictional drug addict and gambler Francis Majcinek or Frankie Machine—a man whose winning way with cards lent him an aura of having a "golden arm"—sent Algren back to his notebooks for an alternative. He liked *Night without Mercy,* which he felt was "a subjective title, carrying emotional overtones, whereas all that *The Man* is is a flat statement of objective fact. . . . Thus I suspect that even though *The Man* is unique, it will not stand up as well, once the novelty of the title has worn off." Algren was wrong; the title became a catchphrase and the novel won a National Book Award. Yet he went through the same tossing and turning with *A Walk on the Wild Side.* Once McCormick approved of it, Algren tried to change it to the bland *Somebody in Boots* and then *Finnerty's Ball.*

⌒

A writer who does cherish his title would probably do well to hold it in reserve and not present it until two or three others, all duds, have been duly rejected, leaving the editor with his editorial honor intact.

CHARLES PORTIS

⌒

CHARLES BAUDELAIRE
The Flowers of Evil (Les Fleurs du Mal) (1857)

SYMBOLIST poet Baudelaire, whose writings embody the decadence of French writing of his era, had planned to call his lush, somewhat sinister poem cycle *Les Limbes,* in an echo of Dante's Limbo on the outskirts of Hell. It is said

that the critic Hippolyte Babou suggested the title *Les Fleurs du Mal* while drinking at a café one night with Baudelaire and other friends, saying that Baudelaire's poems were not only a blossoming of evil, but their beautiful language turned evil into a deceptive and dangerous beauty.

꙳

SAMUEL BECKETT
Waiting for Godot (1952)

"*I*F GODOT were God," dramatist and Irish expatriate Samuel Beckett once said, "I would have called him that." Beckett never publicly commented on the enigma of his play's title, and as a result there is a virtual cottage industry of title and character explorers determined to impose their own brand of order on one of the twentieth century's most interesting plays.

Beckett, who lived most of his adult life in France, wrote his play in French; in French "Godot" does not sound at all like the French word for God, "dieu." He did say once, perhaps in jest, that the name came to him because of the French slang for *boot*, "godillot" or "godasse," as feet play a certain role in his drama. Another possible inspiration, which Beckett never denied, was the day he ran into a large group of people on a street corner watching the annual Tour de France bicycle race. Upon his asking what they were doing, the crowd responded, "We're waiting for Godot"—Godot being the oldest (and slowest) competitor in the race. And yet another story is that as Beckett was waiting for a bus at the corner of the rue Godot de Mauroy, a Parisian street famed for its prostitutes, he was approached by one of the ladies who, when he rejected her, asked irritably whom he was saving himself for—was he "waiting for Godot," as in the street's name. The incongruity of the prostitute's comment struck him as he was writing his play, and he appropriated it as his title.

꒰

> You'll find a title and it will have a certain excitement for you; it will evoke the book, it will push you along. Eventually, you will use it up and you will have to choose another title. When you find the one that doesn't get used up, that's the title you go with.
>
> E. L. DOCTOROW

꒰

SAUL BELLOW
Seize the Day (1956)

NOBEL Prize winner Bellow chose a well-known Latin saying to illustrate his novel of disillusionment. As protagonist Tommy Wilhelm gradually loses everything he holds dear—his family, his job, his dwelling—he finds his hopes for a meaningful life grow weaker and weaker until he is finally stripped of his last possessions by a swindler. Latin poet Horace's warning is an apt reminder of modern man's prospects: Seize the day, put no trust in tomorrow! (*Carpe diem, quam minimum credula postero*—*Odes.*)

⤐

> Sometimes people give titles to me, and sometimes I
> see them on a billboard.   ROBERT PENN WARREN

⤐

PETER BENCHLEY
Jaws (1974)

*P*ETER Benchley remembers that "*Jaws* was the last,
desperate compromise between me and my editor some
twenty minutes before the book had to go to press. I had
fiddled with a hundred alternatives, more or less: *Great
White, The Shark, Leviathan Rising, The Jaws of Death;* a few
Françoise Sagan rip-offs, like *A Silence in the Water;* and a
few helpful suggestions from my father [writer Nathaniel
Benchley], to wit: *What's That Noshin' on My Laig?* At last,
my editor and I agreed that we didn't like any of the
suggested titles, and, in fact, the only *word* we liked in any
permutation was 'jaws.' I recall saying something to the
effect of, 'Screw it, then, let's call it *Jaws,*' and my editor
saying something like, 'Okay, what the hell . . .' My father
didn't like it; my agent didn't like it; my wife didn't like it;
and I didn't much like it. But the bottom line was, who
cares? Nobody reads first novels anyway."

⮎

> Everyone needs an editor.
>
> TIM FOOTE, commenting in *Time* magazine on the fact that Hitler's original title for *Mein Kampf* was *Four-and-a-Half Years of Struggle against Lies, Stupidity, and Cowardice.*

⮎

ROY BLOUNT, JR.

"*I* WORRY about titles quite a bit, while I am writing the books and long after they have gone out of print. Just the other day I was wishing that I had called my first book something else. Its title is *About Three Bricks Shy of a Load*. It came out twenty years ago. *Two Bricks Short of a Lot* is about as close as anybody ever comes to getting it right. Later I brought out an expanded version called *About Three Bricks Shy ... And the Load Filled Up*. One of that title's several drawbacks is that it contains internal punctuation, as do two other titles of mine: *Now, Where Were We?* and *Camels Are Easy, Comedy's Hard*. The only advantage to titles with internal punctuation is that when you list them together, they look like twice as many books.

"I have a weakness for subtitles. Occasionally I see in print that I am the author of *One Fell Soup* and *I'm Just a Bug on the Windshield of Life*, which are the title and the subtitle of the same book—which I wanted to call *The Family Jewels*,

but women employees of the publisher objected. Then I wanted to call it *Mixed Company*, but there was another book (about women in the military) coming out with that title. It is now the name of my ex-wife's theater company.

"The title of mine I like best is that of my worst-selling book, a sort of illustrated meditation on the semiotics of hair. Jim Fitzgerald of Doubleday was the editor. He and I had just about settled on another title—I've forgotten what it was, now, but let's say it was *Human Plumage*. We were discussing it by phone.

" 'I'm liking *Human Plumage* more and more,' he said.

" 'Yeah,' I said. 'It grows on you.'

"Eureka! The perfect title for a book on hair! *It Grows on You*, we called it. I don't know what we should have called it, but just off the top of my head . . . Hey! Too late now.

"The best-fitting title I have ever come up with is that of my seventh book, *Not Exactly What I Had in Mind*. I wish it were more succinct, though.

"My only one-word title is *Crackers*. Today I looked back at my working papers to see what titles I rejected for that book, because I know there were many, including *There Be Alligators*, *Trash No More*, and *The Redneck White House Blues*. Well, my working papers are a jumble, but I did find the original typescript title page. *Crackers* is the title submitted. Gordon Lish, who edited that book for Knopf, was dissatisfied. Scribbled all over the title page are suggestions in Lish's hand.

" 'Title: List a la Farber,' says one: '*Crackers, Carters, Homos, Yids, Country Singers, Reporters. . . .*' Lish liked a book by Manny Farber whose title consisted of a long list of matters dealt with. Indeed my book touched upon questions of ethnicity and sexuality raised during the Carter administration, but I can assure you that neither *Homo* nor *Yid* reflected either the tone of my remarks or their substance. I can also assure you that anybody who thinks I would entertain such a title is crazy; but my book called for crazy editing, up to a point.

"Lish's second scribbled suggestion was *I Seen It Done,* which alluded to a story in the book (about the old boy who, when asked if he believed in infant baptism, said, 'Believe in it? Hell, I've seen it done!'), but which seemed to me too crackerish by half. (This evidently did not strike Lish as a problem, and yet he rejected as my author photograph a picture of me holding two dogs.) His third was *People on Elevators,* which makes absolutely no sense to me now and I feel certain made no sense at all to me then, either. Maybe it's a note Lish made to himself about an entirely different book that he felt needed to be written.

"On the back of that title page I see a host of my own scribbled title alternatives, which make me shudder. Here are three of the *least* silly:

- *Ritzy Crackers*
- *Jimmy, Cracker Scorn and I Declare*
- *The James Earl Carter Jr. Crackro-American Crypto-Peckerwood Revenge*

"At one point Lish called me excitedly with what he regarded as just the thing: *Revenge of the Redheaded Stepchild.* As I recall, my response (which might well make an appropriate title for all too many of my books) was 'Huh?'

"Finally I said I just wanted to stick with *Crackers*.

"At that point Lish revealed that another author had submitted to him a manuscript entitled *Crackers*.

"Tough, I said.

"We did add a subtitle: *This Whole Many-Angled Thing of Jimmy, More Carters, Ominous Little Animals, Sad-Singing Women, My Daddy and Me.* At the last minute, too late I guess to change the subtitle, we dropped the chapter on sad-singing women because Loretta Lynn wouldn't give permission to quote her lyrics.

"The other author who wanted dibs on *Crackers*, according to Lish, and who shall remain nameless, has reviewed several of my subsequent books nastily.

"Someday I hope to write a song with the title 'My Company's Sending Me to Memory School (And All I Want to Do Is Forget).' "

≈

EMILY BRONTË
Wuthering Heights (1847)

IT has puzzled school-age readers for 150 years. Just what does "wuthering" mean? Brontë explains the enigmatic word in the first chapter of her brooding Gothic tale: "Wuthering Heights is the name of Mr. Heathcliff's dwelling. 'Wuthering' being a significant provincial adjective, descriptive of the atmospheric tumult to which its station is exposed in stormy weather. Pure, bracing ventilation theyst have up there, at all times, indeed: one may guess the power of the north wind, blowing over the edge, by the excessive slant of a few stunted firs at the end of the house . . ."

20

≋

DEE BROWN
Bury My Heart at Wounded Knee (1971)

*H*ISTORIAN Dee Brown found his title for his tragic history of the conquest of the American West and the eradication of the Native American tribes in "American Names," a poem by Stephen Vincent Benét. Here are the first and last stanzas:

> I have fallen in love with American names,
> The sharp names that never get fat,
> The snakeskin-titles of mining claims,
> The plumed war-bonnet of Medicine Hat,
> Tucson and Deadwood and Lost Mule Flat.
>
> . . .
>
> I shall not rest quiet in Montparnasse.
> I shall not lie easy in Winchelsea.
> You may bury my body in Sussex grass,
> You may bury my tongue at Champmedy.
> I shall not be there. I shall rise and pass.
> Bury my heart at Wounded Knee.

≋

HELEN GURLEY BROWN
Sex and the Single Woman (1962)

*H*ELEN Gurley Brown, longtime editor of the magazine *Cosmopolitan*, invented the concept of the sexually liberated "Cosmo girl." Her first book was a sensation. It immediately hit the best-seller lists and helped millions of

women understand that they could have a valid and exciting identity beyond that of wife or mother. "I knew I wanted to write a book about sex being okay for single women," Brown has said. "I knew that going *in* and so the book was created along those lines. Originally I called it *Sex for the Single Woman* but everyone felt that was too 'immoral' (as though I was *promoting* sex among these people) so I cleaned it up and called it *Sex and the Single Woman.*"

⌒

ELIZABETH BARRETT BROWNING
Sonnets from the Portuguese (1850)

*T*HE moving love poems in *Sonnets from the Portuguese* were written by Browning to her husband, poet Robert Browning, and were never intended for a wider audience. Robert Browning insisted they be published because, he said, "I dared not keep to myself the finest Sonnets written in any language since Shakespeare's." The poems are not a translation from Portuguese; it is thought they are so called because Browning's pet name for his dark-complexioned wife was "my little Portuguese."

TITLES WE'RE GLAD GOT CHANGED

The Mute was changed to *The Heart Is a Lonely Hunter*

At This Point in Time was changed to *All the President's Men*

Private Fleming, His Various Battles was changed to *The Red Badge of Courage*

23

Judah: A Tale of the Christ was changed to *Ben-Hur*

Before This Anger was changed to *Roots*

First Impressions was changed to *Pride and Prejudice*

Couples and Houses and Days was changed to *Couples*

To Climb the Wall was changed to *The Blackboard Jungle*

The House of the Faith was changed to *Brideshead Revisited*

The Birds and the Bees was changed to *Everything You Always Wanted to Know about Sex *But Were Afraid to Ask*

It Shouldn't Happen to a Vet was changed to *All Things Bright and Beautiful*

They Don't Build Statues to Businessmen was changed to *Valley of the Dolls*

The Kingdom by the Sea was changed to *Lolita*

⌐

ANTHONY BURGESS
A Clockwork Orange (1962)

"CLOCKWORK oranges don't exist," Burgess once said, discussing his notorious ode to violence, "except in the speech of old Londoners." For such people, the saying "queer as a clockwork orange" meant that a person was bizarre and outrageous. "Europeans who translated the title as *Arancia a Orologeria* or *Orange Méchanique* could not understand its Cockney resonance and they assumed it meant a hand grenade, a cheaper kind of explosive pineapple. I mean it to stand for the application of a mechanistic

24

morality to a living organism oozing with juice and sweetness."

✑

> In 1939 Philadelphia publisher J. B. Lippincott issued George Stevens's *Lincoln's Doctor's Dog & Other Famous Best Sellers*. An analysis of the phenomenon of best-sellers, it took its title from the three then most commercial subjects selling in bookstores. Forty years later, a Canadian publisher imitated the joke by publishing *Hitler, Golf and Cats*. What would today's surefire best-selling title reflect?

✑

WILLIAM BURROUGHS
Naked Lunch (1959)

*J*ACK Kerouac is thought to have coined the phrase which Beat novelist Burroughs applied to his surreal vision of an American underculture. When asked what it really meant, Burroughs said, "The title means exactly what the words say. NAKED lunch—a frozen moment when everyone sees what is on the end of every fork."

✑

> "Each had his past shut in him like the leaves of a book known to him by heart; and his friends could only read the title." VIRGINIA WOOLF, *Jacob's Room*

∾

SAMUEL BUTLER
The Way of All Flesh (1903)

*O*RIGINALLY called *Ernest Pontifex*, after the awkward young hero of this posthumously published novel, it is the saga of four generations of a family given to much bad luck. Good fortune smiles in the end, and Butler found a passage from the Bible to symbolize his tale. Here, "flesh" is substituted for "earth" in the 1609 English Catholic Bible's Joshua: "And, behold, this day I am going the way of all the earth; and ye know in all your hearts and in all your souls, that not one thing hath failed of all the good things which the LORD your God spake concerning you."

∾

JAMES M. CAIN
The Postman Always Rings Twice (1934)

*M*ADE into a play, two movies, and an opera, newspaperman Cain's first novel, a steamy and sordid tale of sexual passion, murder, and double-crossing, has a memorable title. Depending on his mood, Cain told two different stories about its genesis. In one he claimed that the mailman would ring his doorbell twice to alert Cain he was delivering bills, and only once if he was bringing a personal letter. The daily delivery of bills drove him wild as he was working on his manuscript—and provided him with heavy symbolism for his novel. In his other version, Cain said that his mailman would ring twice whenever he was delivering a manuscript of Cain's that had been rejected by a publisher

and returned to the author. Cain was rejected so often he came to expect the mailman to ring twice every day. One day he rang only once—Alfred Knopf had taken his book on for publication. To celebrate, Cain named his novel for his days of struggle.

꙰

Most difficult book title to remember:
  YMA, AVA, YMA, ABBA, YMA, OONA, YMA, IDA,
YMA, AGA AND OTHERS
  by Thomas Meehan

꙰

LEWIS CARROLL
Alice's Adventures in Wonderland (1865)

O N July 4, 1862, the Reverend Charles Lutwidge Dodgson, then a mathematics professor at Oxford but later known by his pen name of Lewis Carroll, went rowing with the three young daughters of the dean of Oxford's Christ Church. Lorina Charlotte, Alice, and Edith had brought a picnic lunch, and as they boated upriver Dodgson—Carroll—spun tales that found an especially enthusiastic audience in Alice, who was ten years old. Such was her enthusiasm that Carroll finally committed to paper her favorite episodes in the magical adventures of a little girl called Alice, and he called the collection *Alice's Adventures Under Ground.* Expanded further, it was finally published under the title now known to the world.

✑

It was Lewis Carroll who first suggested to his publisher that the dust jacket carry the title of the book.
Thus Carroll's *The Hunting of the Snark* was the first
book to be published with a printed jacket.

✑

JOYCE CARY
The Horse's Mouth (1944)

*E*NGLISH author Arthur Joyce Cary had already become
well known for his highly individual writing style
before he published what was to be his most famous book,
"a damn queer book" he called it, "but to hell with the
publisher." His tale of painter Gulley Jimson's raffish adventures in a larger-than-life London was fought over by several
publishers. The winner, Harper Brothers, had serious
doubts about the title, though, and thought something
different might be better for sales. Cary's reply sums up
many writers' feelings of frustration with their publisher:
"The point is that my titles are essential parts of the book. I
don't forget for a moment that they appear at the top of
each page . . . the Horse's Mouth is not merely Gulley, it
is the mysterious injunction laid upon such as Gulley to
sacrifice their lives and comforts for line and form and
colour—and always new forms, new lines . . . I think a
change [of title] runs the danger of being misunderstood as
a failure of comprehension."

⮌

> Translators, mistaking my simplicity for insubstantiality, render me superficial I am told. *Tiens.* In German they thought to make my *La Difficulté d'Etre* "the difficulty to *Leben*"; no! "the difficulty *zu sein.*" The difficulty to live is another thing: taxes, complications, and all the rest. But the difficulty to *be*—ah! to be here; to exist.   JEAN COCTEAU

⮌

RAYMOND CHANDLER
Farewell, My Lovely (1940)

NOIR master Raymond Chandler intended to call his new Philip Marlowe novel *The Second Murderer*, after a scene in Shakespeare's *King Richard III* in which Richard sends two hired killers to drown his brother Clarence, thus clearing his own way to the throne. The second murderer begins to have scruples about killing in cold blood, but gets down to business upon being reminded of the cash reward that awaits them both. Given that his novel was about police corruption, the evocation of cowardly greed pleased Chandler greatly. His publisher, Alfred Knopf, preferred to look elsewhere for inspiration, and liked *Sweet Bells Jangle*, from Ophelia's description of an apparently mad Hamlet. Chandler detested the idea—it seemed like literary pretension—and came back with the only partly tongue-in-cheek *Zounds, He Dies*. Knopf wisely backed down and let Chandler abandon Shakespeare entirely—they were getting nowhere—for a tough-sounding, edgy line of dialogue instead.

TITLES FROM SHAKESPEARE

Brave New World

Pale Fire

The Dogs of War

The Winter of Our Discontent

Remembrance of Things Past

Summer's Lease

Rosencrantz and Guildenstern Are Dead

The Sound and the Fury

Something Wicked This Way Comes

Cakes and Ale

Ape and Essence

Raymond Chandler, who invented some of the most haunting titles in American fiction, kept long lists of title possibilities in his notebooks. Among the titles he never used are *The Corpse Came in Person, A Few May Remember, The Man with the Shredded Ear, Zone of Twilight, Parting before Danger, The Is to Was Man, All Guns Are Loaded, Return from Ruin, Lament but No Tears, Too Late to Sleep,* and *The Cool-Off.* He told Alfred Knopf how much he disliked "titles like *The Strange Case of* or *The*

Puzzle of or *The Mystery of* for the reason that I think they put too much emphasis on the mystery itself, and I have not the ingenuity to devise the sort of intricate and recondite puzzle the purest aficionados go for. The title might lead them to expect a type of story they are not getting."

≈

RAYMOND CHANDLER
The High Window (1942)

CHANDLER was working on two novels simultaneously: *The Brasher Doubloon* and *The Lady in the Lake*. Work on both was fitful as he and his wife moved from apartment to apartment, ever searching for the perfect place to live. To keep himself from tinkering with it any longer, Chandler sent the manuscript of *The Brasher Doubloon* off to his publisher, who as usual loved the book but hated the title and who wrote back to Chandler that booksellers would pronounce "brasher" as "brassiere." Chandler explained that a brasher was a late-eighteenth-century coin, but then agreed that booksellers' needs came first. "How about *The High Window*?" he suggested. "It is simple, suggestive, and points to the ultimate essential clue."

≈

While finishing *The Lady in the Lake* Raymond Chandler wrote to his publisher, "I'm trying to think up a good title for you to want me to change."

❧

WILKIE COLLINS
The Woman in White (1860)

*W*ILKIE Collins, who wrote the first full-length detective stories in English, was immensely popular as a novelist in Victorian England. As he worked for weeks and then months on what was to become his most famous tale, *The Woman in White*, he was unable to find a suitable title and fell into a deep funk. One evening, as he lay on the grass gazing at a lighthouse near his home, he recalled the opening of his book, in which "a solitary Woman, dressed from head to foot in white," appears suddenly on a road drenched in moonlight to change the destiny of a startled stranger hurrying home. In desperation Collins used the image as his title, but not before asking his friend Charles Dickens for his opinion. "I have not the slightest doubt," Dickens responded, "that *The Woman in White* is the name of names, and very title of titles."

❧

EVAN CONNELL
Mrs. Bridge (1959)

*W*HEN Evan Connell first began writing his novel that would become a cult classic, he remembered a socially prominent woman in his native Kansas City named India Edwards. *India* as a name attracted him, although it would be an unusual choice for the conventional midwestern matron Connell had in mind. As he considered the family he was writing about, the last name of Bridge seemed possible—with its overtones of a bridge-playing country club society, and the implication that one can avoid much social unpleasantness by simply ignoring it, by crossing the abyss of unpleasantness on a bridge. Connell's agent suggested he call it *The File on India Bridge*, which to him sounded too clinical. Connell preferred the clean straightforward lines of *Mrs. Bridge*, which was such a success it was followed ten years later by *Mr. Bridge*.

᠅

DON DELILLO
White Noise (1985)

$\mathcal{T}$HIS brilliant and unnerving comic novel explores the almost religious paranoia, dread, and superstition that paradoxically underlie the technological, message-laden surface of American consumer culture. Throughout the book dozens of advertising slogans, brand names, catchphrases, instructions, trademarks, and corporate titles are repeated, by way of evoking the ceaseless barrage of messages that assault us today. Overly familiar verbal formulas take on the feeling of mantras or prayers. One of them is "Panasonic," and the name of the giant Japanese electronics manufacturer served as the original title of DeLillo's novel. The name evoked both the noise of contemporary culture ("sonic") and its inescapability ("Pan-"). However, the lawyers for Panasonic objected to the use of the title of their corporation on trademark infringement grounds. So the publisher and DeLillo retreated to the safer *White Noise*, a term derived from astrophysics and broadcasting for the meaningless but omnipresent electronic signals that suffuse the cosmos and the airwaves. It won the 1985 National Book Award for fiction.

≈

NELSON DeMILLE

*T*he best-selling author notes that "titles have always been a major problem for me, and in this era of international publishing, many titles don't translate or travel well. For instance, my British publisher was unhappy with *The Talbot Odyssey*, because the Talbot is a British car, a rather bad car, and they pointed out, 'Would you want a book in America called *The Edsel Odyssey*?' Oddly enough, they went with it anyway. *The Gold Coast* presented another problem, as in most of Europe the Gold Coast refers exclusively to the African Gold Coast, while in America we have many Gold Coasts, the connotation being a wealthy area near the shore. The Germans absolutely refused to use the title and called the book *In Der Kalte Der Nacht (In the Cold of the Night)*. The other European publishers decided to go with a literal translation, hoping that the cover art and blurbs would clarify the title to the extent that readers didn't think it was about Africa. Incidentally, I had played around with other titles for this Gatsby-esque tale, such as *The North Shore* and *The Green Light*, but in the end I went with *The Gold Coast* and damn the confusion. *By the Rivers of Babylon*, being biblical, was a snap for everyone except the Japanese, who asked how many rivers there were in Babylon. *Word of Honor* concerns a court-martial, and the title seems apt, but half of the letters I get call it *World of Honor*. *The Charm School* was originally called *The Finishing School*.

Unfortunately, another big book with that title came out just before mine [by Gail Godwin] and I had to change it at the last minute. But I always remember what an old editor said to me: the title of a best-selling novel is the title of a best-selling novel."

↷

CHARLES DICKENS
Bleak House (1853)

*D*ICKENS's ninth novel, about the never-ending, self-perpetuating court case known as *Jarndyce and Jarndyce*, was published in monthly installments over the course of a year and a half. Apparently the author wrestled with a title for much of that time; the Victoria and Albert Museum in London holds the original manuscript of the work, which includes such title ideas as *Tom-All-Alone's The Ruined House, Bleak House Academy, The East Wind, Tom-All-Alone's The Ruined Mill,* and *Tom-All-Alone's Factory that Got Into Chancery and Never Got Out.*

↷

Among the names Dickens toyed with before settling on *Martin Chuzzlewit* (1844) were *Martin Sweetledew, Martin Chuzzletoe, Martin Sweetleback,* and *Martin Sweetlewag.*

≈

CHARLES DICKENS
Hard Times (1854)

*D*ICKENS had no sooner finished writing *Bleak House* in August of 1853 than he started on what was to become *Hard Times*. As ever with this prolific author, it took him some time before he was able to settle on a title. Making up a list of possibilities, he sent it to his editor, asking him to look at the suggestions "between this and two o'clock or so, when I will call. It is my usual day, you observe, on which I have jotted them down—Friday! It seems to me that there are three very good ones among them. I should like to know whether you hit upon the same." We don't know which three Dickens liked so much, but we do know the plethora of ideas he gave his editor: *According to Cocker, Prove It, Stubborn Things, Mr. Gradgrind's Facts, The Grindstone, Two and Two Are Four, Something Tangible, Our Hardheaded Friend, Rust and Dust, Simple Arithmetic, A Matter of Calculation, A Mere Question of Figures*, and *The Gradgrind Philosophy*, as well as *Hard Times*. Dickens also toyed with *Fact, Hard-headed Gradgrind, Hard Heads and Soft Hearts, Heads and Tales*, and *Black and White*.

≈

THEODORE DREISER
Sister Carrie (1900)

*A*T the turn of the century Dreiser and his wife were living in an apartment on West 102nd Street in New York City. Dreiser's friend Arthur Henry, newly arrived in

New York from Ohio, lived with them too, and hoped to launch a literary career. Henry began work on a novel, and urged Dreiser, then a reporter, to start writing as well, so that they could work together and encourage each other. Dreiser was initially reluctant, but Henry kept at it. Dreiser later remembered, "Finally, I took out a piece of yellow paper and to please him wrote down a title at random— *Sister Carrie.* . . . My mind was a blank except for the name. I had no idea who or what she was to be. I have often thought there was something mystic about it, as if I were being used, like a medium."

～

THEODORE DREISER
An American Tragedy (1925)

*F*ROM the very first page of his sensational tale (based on a true story) of failed romance and brutal murder, Dreiser had his title firmly in mind. But his publisher, the flamboyant Horace Liveright, didn't care for it at all, preferring to name the novel after Dreiser's protagonist. As a title, *Griffiths* (for the weak-willed murderer Clyde Griffiths) struck Dreiser as a terrible idea. Liveright begged him to change his mind, or at least the name of his character: "I feel I must once more implore you," Liveright wrote, "to call the book *Ewing* or *Warner* or some other good representative name. . . . Commercial, I may appear, but in the end it is you who will keep after me if the book doesn't sell." Dreiser could not be swayed, feeling that a simple name lacked best-selling appeal, and insisted on the epic sweep of his original title.

≈

GEORGE ELIOT
The Mill on the Floss (1860)

*F*AR from the tumult of modern publishing, Eliot's genteel correspondence with John Blackwood, her publisher, regarding a title for her novel of rural mores evokes a strong nostalgia for a different age. "We are demurring about a title," she wrote at the end of 1859, "having considered and discarded *St. Ogg's on the Floss*. [We] prefer *The House of Tulliver* to our old notion of *Sister Maggie*. It has the advantage of slipping easily off the lazy English tongue, but it is after too common a fashion (*The Newcomes*, *The Bertrams*, etc.). Then, there is *The Tulliver Family*. Pray meditate and give us your opinion." After a few days Blackwood responded. "It suddenly came across me that *The Mill on the Floss* would be an appropriate title and in some respects more appropriate and curiously exciting than any of those suggested. It has too a sort of poetical sound." In the face of such inspiration Eliot graciously assented, wary only of the "rather laborious utterance" of Blackwood's idea. To be sure Eliot was happy with his title, Blackwood had both potential titles printed up as samples. Eliot examined them both and found *The Mill on the Floss* more pleasing to the eye than *The House of Tulliver*, and therefore the title of choice.

≈

The great critic and editor Irving Howe won a National Book Award in 1976 for his moving history of Eastern European Jewish immigration to the United States, *World of Our Fathers*. One evening, during a lecture he was giving on the book, a woman criticized him for not titling the book *World of Our Fathers and Mothers*. "*World of Our Fathers* is a title," he returned. "*World of Our Fathers and Mothers* is a speech."

꒰

WILLIAM FAULKNER
Absalom, Absalom! (1936)

CONSIDERED by many to be Faulkner's most difficult and complex novel, this tale of the Old South was to be called *Dark House*, to symbolize the hidden nature of Southern identity. Narrated by the sensitive Quentin Compson (who appeared in *The Sound and the Fury*), *Absalom* tells of a man's efforts to establish a plantation dynasty in the pre– Civil War South, and how his efforts are brought to ruin by his own sons. Faulkner turned to the Bible for his tale's title, and found his source in 2 Samuel, in the tragic story of Absalom and his father, King David: "Would God I had died for thee, O Absalom, my son, my son!"

꒰

William Faulkner had originally planned to call a novel *The Cross: A Fable*, which would have been shown as a rebus on the title page. His publishers objected, however, that librarians had no way of

listing rebuses alphabetically in their card catalogs,
and so the book became simply *A Fable*.

⤸

WILLIAM FAULKNER
Light in August (1932)

COMMENTING on the title of his tale of poor whites and
racial hatred in the South, Faulkner said, "It has in a
sense nothing to do with the book at all." *Dark House*, which
Faulkner also wanted to use for *Absalom, Absalom!*, was the
working title, but the author wasn't satisfied with it. He
found his muse in a chance remark of his wife's that the
light in August in the South had a peculiar quality and was
different from light anywhere else. Faulkner liked the image
and whimsically took it as his title.

⤸

WILLIAM FAULKNER
The Sound and the Fury (1929)

FAULKNER's cinematic take on the Compson family, one
of the great clans of his fictional Yoknapatawpha
County now fallen on hard times, is shocking because only
after a few pages does the reader realize the story is narrated
by an idiot. Originally the entire story was to be told
by Benjy Compson—who could describe what he saw
happening but could not understand it—but Faulkner
understood no one would be able to read his book. And so

Benjy's two brothers in turn take over the narration. *Macbeth* gave Faulkner his title, in Act V:

MACBETH: Out, out, brief candle!
                Life's but a walking shadow, a poor player
                That struts and frets his hour upon the stage,
                And then is heard no more; it is a tale
                Told by an idiot, full of sound and fury,
                Signifying nothing.

⤳

F. SCOTT FITZGERALD
The Great Gatsby (1925)

*F*ITZGERALD's superb novel of marital infidelity and life among the very rich has come to epitomize the "Jazz Age" of the 1920s; the title alone evokes straw boaters and the mansions of Long Island, striped suits, Prohibition-era cocktails, and endless parties. And as a title it seems perfect. But throughout 1924, as Scribner's was preparing his book for publication, Fitzgerald worried endlessly to his editor, Maxwell Perkins, about the book's title. His favorite choice was *Trimalchio in West Egg* (Trimalchio was the rich patron in Petronius's *Satyricon*). Perkins objected and Fitzgerald invented other titles: *Gold-hatted Gatsby* and *The High-bouncing Lover* recurred in his increasingly frantic correspondence. Ring Lardner declared *Trimalchio* to be unpronounceable. Perkins thought *The Great Gatsby* too much like *Babbitt*. Fitzgerald was never able to feel comfortable with any title for his novel, and even after *The Great Gatsby* was published wrote to Perkins lamenting that he had not chosen *Trimalchio in West Egg*.

Among J. P. Donleavy's wordy titles:
Meet My Maker, the Mad Molecule
The Saddest Summer of Samuel S.
The Beastly Beatitudes of Balthazar B.
The Destinies of Darcy Dancer

≈

FORD MADOX FORD
The Good Soldier (1915)

*T*HE English expatriate Ford Madox Ford (born Ford Hermann Hueffer) was known for his dour outlook on life and his strained relationships with other writers, whom he saw as competitors. He had originally planned to publish what was later recognized as his masterpiece, a four-sided love story, under the title *The Saddest Story* (an apt description). But 1915 was a low point for the English during World War I, and so to boost patriotism and national spirit his publishers persuaded him to adopt a more positive and patriotic title—despite the complete absence of military subject matter in the book.

≈

It is not true that the avant-garde poet E. E. Cummings never capitalized the letters of his name. He did, however, give his books highly unusual titles, including *&, XLI Poems, HIM, W(ViVa), No Thanks, 1 x 1, CIOPW* (for charcoal, ink, oils, pencil, water-

color), and *i:SIX NONLECTURES*. In 1930 he published a book with no title at all.

‌

> E. M. FORSTER
> **Where Angels Fear to Tread** (1905)

*E*NGLISH essayist and novelist Forster submitted his
first book to *Blackwood's Magazine*, hoping they would
publish this work by an unknown writer in installments.
Instead, *Blackwood's* offered to publish the entire novel at
once, balking only at Forster's choice for a title: *Monteriano*,
after the Italian town that serves as the novel's setting. It
seemed too foreign a name, and thus not pleasing. Instead
they suggested either *From a Sense of Duty* or *Where Angels Fear
to Tread*, the latter phrase coming from a line in Alexander
Pope's "Essay on Criticism": "For fools rush in where angels
fear to tread." Forster, eager to be published, chose *Angels*
but never felt quite comfortable with it, even to the point
of crossing it out on the title page when he sent a copy of
the finished book to Leonard and Virginia Woolf. *The
Manchester Guardian*, in reviewing the book, disliked it as
well, calling the title "mawkish, sentimental and commonplace."

‌

This space is usually reserved for a brief description
of a book's contents. In this case, however, I must
admit frankly that I do not know what Miss Stein is
talking about. I do not even understand the title.

Publisher BENNETT CERF's signed copy on the dust
jacket of Gertrude Stein's *The Geographical History of
America or the Relation of Human Nature to the Human
Mind* (1936)

᠊ᢈ

GAIL GODWIN

*G*AIL Godwin is one of America's most distinguished
contemporary novelists. Here she shares her thoughts
on her own book titles: "Two of the titles originated with
the idea of the book and were inextricable with the material
throughout: *The Finishing School* (1985) and *A Southern Family*
(1987). *Glass People* (1972) is the only title given to me by
someone else. When a friend read the manuscript, which
was then titled *Suspended Woman*, he said, 'These people are
both as brittle and delicate as glass, and they're always
looking in mirrors, in one way or another! They're like . . .
glass people.'

"*Father Melancholy's Daughter* (1991) was *Vinca* until I was
flying into Chattanooga for a writer's festival and wishing I
had a better title. I was meditating on this while staring at
the back of Walker Percy's head (he was several seats in
front of me) when the words formed themselves and I knew
they were perfect. (My [former] publisher, however, didn't
agree. He sent word that *Father Melancholy's Daughter* 'sure
doesn't shout Big Book to me.' I sent word back that it
wasn't a shouting book and to think of it as a small book if
it would make him feel any better.)

"The novel I am about to finish (1993) was called *Miseri-*

cord until—once again—flying in an airplane and wishing I had a better title, I thought of the perfect title: *The Good Husband.* (When I recently sent my assistant to photocopy some chapters, she came back and reported that a woman had looked over her shoulder, seen the title page, and snorted, 'Ha! Where? Let me know when you find him.')"

≈

SUE GRAFTON
"A" Is for Alibi (1982)

*I*N 1982 Sue Grafton published her first Kinsey Millhone mystery, *"A" Is for Alibi.* When she followed alphabetical sequence with her second novel, *"B" Is for Burglar,* she started one of the great guessing games of modern book publishing—would she go all the way through the alphabet, and what would the books all be called? To date Grafton has published, in addition to the two books cited, *"C" Is for Corpse, "D" Is for Deadbeat, "E" Is for Evidence, "F" Is for Fugitive, "G" Is for Gumshoe, "H" Is for Homicide, "I" Is for Innocent,* and *"J" Is for Judgment.* Her savvy publisher held a contest for "J," inviting readers and booksellers nationwide to guess the new title. Among the entries were Jury, Jeopardy, Jung, Jalapeño, Jojoba, and Jell-O. How did Grafton get started writing such titles? "I was always interested in mysteries with linking or related titles since my father, C. W. Grafton, based the only two of his unfinished series on a children's nursery rhyme about an old lady trying to get her pig over a stile (*The Rat Began to Gnaw the Rope, The Rope Began to Hang the Butcher*). I'd long been a fan of John D. MacDonald whose titles were linked by color, and Harry Kemelman whose titles were linked by days of the week. One day I was perusing a book of cartoons by Edward Gorey, who published a series of pen and ink drawings of little Victorian children 'done in' by various means . . . 'B is for Basil devoured by Bears' . . . 'K is for Kate killed with an Axe.' I could feel a cartoon light bulb form above my head and I thought to myself . . . gee, why couldn't you do a series of crime novels based on the alphabet?" Grafton has already settled on a title for her final Millhone book: "Z" Is for Zero. She used to think that after completing the alphabet she would move on to books with numbers in the title, but with sixteen books to go, retirement is a welcome option.

꩜

What many consider to be the greatest series of mysteries ever written—John D. MacDonald's Travis McGee books—all include a color in the title. Mac-Donald did so as a mnemonic device to help readers avoid buying the same book twice—an experience all too common among hungry mystery addicts. The McGee books are *The Deep Blue Goodbye, Nightmare in Pink, A Purple Place for Dying, The Quick Red Fox, A Deadly Shade of Gold, Bright Orange for the Shroud, Darker than Amber, One Fearful Yellow Eye, Pale Gray for Guilt, The Girl in the Plain Brown Wrapper, Dress Her in Indigo, The Long Lavender Look, A Tan and Sandy Silence, The Scarlet Ruse, The Turquoise Lament, The Dreadful Lemon Sky, The Empty Copper Sea, The Green Ripper, Free Fall in Crimson, Cinnamon Skin,* and *The Lonely Silver Rain.* MacDonald was about to start a new McGee novel which included "Ginger" in the title when he died. There is a long-standing rumor among publishing people that there exists, somewhere in a locked cabinet, a final McGee adventure in which the moody, quixotic salvage consultant meets his end. It is called *A Black Border for McGee*.

ᗱ

ALLAN GURGANUS
Oldest Living Confederate Widow Tells All (1989)

*I*N the summer of 1982, when southern writer Gurganus was working at Yaddo, the writer's colony, he read a brief item in the *New York Times* noting that a few widows of Confederate soldiers were still alive—120 years after the war—and were receiving pensions from the government. The *Times* included the phrase "oldest living Confederate widow." When Gurganus saw that, he was galvanized. "I was on my way to swim, but instead I went back to my room and typed for four hours. When I stood up, I had written the first 30 pages of the novel . . . I thought it would be a 35-page story, then a novella of 100 pages. Twelve hundred manuscript pages later, I realized it was not just Lucy's story, it was everybody's story."

≈

DASHIELL HAMMETT
Red Harvest (1929)

*M*YSTERY master Hammett's first novel, after years of writing pulp stories for magazines like *Black Mask* and working as a private detective, was initially called *Poisonville*. His eventual publisher, Alfred Knopf, who also published James M. Cain and Raymond Chandler, was notorious for challenging authors on their book title choices. He found *Poisonville* "hopeless" as a title, and set Hammett to work finding something better. Hammett tried and tossed out *The Seventeenth Murder, Murder Plus, The Wilsson Matter, The City of Death, The Cleansing of Poisonville,* and *The Black City* before thinking of *Red Harvest,* which evoked both left-wing radicalism and the flow of blood. When booksellers agreed with Knopf that *Poisonville* was in fact "hopeless" and *Red Harvest* a much more interesting choice, Hammett agreed to the change.

≈

The Prizzi books were titled from a town in northwestern Sicily, Prizzi, and the sardonic application of that in which the Mafia had no interest: Honor, Family, Glory.　　　　RICHARD CONDON

∽

DASHIELL HAMMETT
The Maltese Falcon (1930)

*H*AMMETT hit on the title for what would become his most enduring detective story right away, even before he had a firm story outline in mind. But as usual, he had trouble with Alfred Knopf about it. "You ought to give a little more thought and worry to your titles," groused the publisher. "Whenever people can't pronounce a title or an author's name, they are, more than you would think, too shy to go into a bookstore and try." Interestingly, Knopf felt the word "Falcon" would be the stumbling block. When Hammett told him that in California people loved his title choices, Knopf snapped, "It doesn't matter what they think in the provinces." Knopf's dislike of Hammett's titles was echoed by Algonquin Round Table regular Dorothy Parker, who noted that Hammett had "a touch of rare genius in his selection of undistinguished titles for his mystery stories."

∽

LORRAINE HANSBERRY
A Raisin in the Sun (1959)

*C*HICAGO-BORN Hansberry wrote the first play by an African-American woman ever produced on Broadway. Winner of the Drama Critics Circle Award, her play describes the efforts of a struggling family to escape ghetto life for the greener pastures of white suburbia. The injustice and intolerance felt by Hansberry's fictional family are best embodied by Langston Hughes's poem "Harlem":

What happens to a dream deferred?
Does it dry up
like a raisin in the sun? . . .
Or does it explode?

❧

The indefatigable Bennett Cerf, best remembered as
the longtime publisher of Random House, told of a
book called *The Ten Commandments* that was to be
published for the armed services during World War II
but was too long. One of Cerf's editors suggested,
"How about using only five of them and calling it *A
Treasury of the World's Best Commandments?*"

❧

THOMAS HARDY
Far from the Madding Crowd (1874)

*H*ARDY's rich novel of the sustaining love Gabriel Oak
and Bathsheba Everdene bear each other amidst the
turbulent passions of their neighbors took its title from
Thomas Gray's 1750 poem "Elegy Written in a Country
Churchyard":

Far from the madding crowd's ignoble strife,
Their wishes never learn'd to stray;
Along the cool sequestered vale of life
They kept the noiseless tenor of their way.

〜

THOMAS HARDY
Jude the Obscure (1895)

*H*ARDY's novel of flesh versus spirit—in which flesh decidedly wins out—shocked his contemporaries with its explicitness. The doomed Jude was created as Jack Head in a story Hardy called *The Simpleton;* Jack was half of an idealistic young couple who seek privacy in a highly moralistic age. As the story developed, Hardy, deliberately evoking the image of Judas Iscariot, changed his hero's name to Jude Fawley and made him a man doomed to life as a pariah. *The Simpleton* changed to *The Recalcitrants,* and then to *Hearts Insurgent,* and as such was published in serial form in *Harper's New Monthly Magazine.* When *Harper's* discovered that it had recently published a work by the same name by another writer, Hardy had to change his title, and his doomed protagonist took center stage.

〜

THOMAS HARDY
Tess of the D'Urbervilles (1891)

*H*ARDY once remarked that he would have called his novel *Tess of the Hardys* if it had not seemed "too personal." Instead he searched for a phrase that would evoke the tragedy of illegitimacy in a literary way: *The Body and Soul of Sue, Too Late, Beloved!, A Daughter of the D'Urbervilles.* Too melodramatic, these were abandoned in short order and Hardy returned to the simple dignity of his tale with a direct allusion to his heroine.

↝

The first miniature book published in America appeared in 1705 and measured 2 by 3½ inches. Printed by William Secker and comprising 92 pages, its title was practically longer than the book itself: *A Wedding Ring Fit for the Finger, or the Salve of Divinity on the Sore of Humanity with directions to those men that want wives, how to choose them; and to those women that have husbands, how to use them.*

↝

ROBERT HEINLEIN
Stranger in a Strange Land (1961)

*T*HE title of Heinlein's now-classic novel, considered by many to be the greatest work of science fiction ever written, has its source in the Bible. It is the tale of a human being, Valentine Michael Smith, who is returned to Earth after being raised by aliens: "And Moses was content to dwell with the man: and he gave Moses Zipporah his daughter. And she bare him a son, and he called his name Gershom: for he said, I have been a stranger in a strange land" (Exodus 2:21–22).

PLANETS AND MOONS IN TITLES
A Moon for the Misbegotten
The Sun Also Rises
The Transit of Venus

The Sirens of Titan
The Good Earth
Two under the Indian Sun
The Moons of Jupiter
Pluto, Animal Lover
Mars & Her Children
Tell Me That You Love Me, Junie Moon

⫝

JOSEPH HELLER
Catch-22 (1961)

*H*ELLER's savage anti-war satire was an immediate success upon publication and remains a milestone in
modern American fiction. The title is so famous on its own
merits that it has become a commonly used phrase in the
English language, signifying something absurdly impossible
to achieve or Kafkaesque in proportion. It started out,
though, as *Catch-18*, and Simon & Schuster would have
published it as such had not rival publisher Doubleday
stepped in. Doubleday was planning publication of best-
selling author Leon Uris's *Mila 18*, and when they heard
that a first novel by an unknown was coming out at the
same time with a similarly numbered title, they firmly
protested. Simon & Schuster in the end acquiesced, and
Heller changed his title to avoid trouble. (Heller's editor
recalled that *Catch-22* had been years in the writing and had
originally been cataloged as *Catch-14!*)

⮐

In 1868 John William DeForest wrote an essay called
"The Great American Novel," in which he suggested
that someone write the definitive novel about the
American experience. Since then, the phrase has been
used jokingly for every budding novelist's manuscript—and for two published novels as well. Clyde
Davis wrote *The Great American Novel* in 1938, a tale of
a newspaperman who tries unsuccessfully to write a
great book by the same title. And in 1973 Philip Roth
published a baseball parody under the same title.

⮐

ERNEST HEMINGWAY
For Whom the Bell Tolls (1940)

A vivid and romantic treatment of the Spanish Civil
War, Hemingway's story of American volunteer Robert
Jordan and his passionate but hopeless love for Spanish
guerrilla Pilar was a plea for awareness of the evils of
totalitarianism. Published as World War II was beginning,
the novel idealizes liberty and action, and Hemingway
found his story's moral best expressed by one of John
Donne's *Devotions*:

No man is an *Iland*, intire of itselfe; every man is a
peece of the *Continent*, a part of the *maine*; if a *Clod* bee

washed away by the *Sea, Europe* is the lesse, as well as if a *Promontorie* were, as well as if a *Mannor* of thy *friends,* or of *thine owne* were; any mans *death* diminishes me, because I am involved in *Mankinde;* and therefore never send to know for whom the *bell* tolls; It tolls for *thee.*

> A good title should be like a good metaphor; it should intrigue without being too baffling or too obvious. WALKER PERCY

> I make a list of titles *after* I've finished the story or book—sometimes as many as a hundred. Then I start eliminating them, sometimes all of them.
> ERNEST HEMINGWAY

ERNEST HEMINGWAY
A Moveable Feast (1964)

*A*LTHOUGH he worked on it intermittently from the 1930s up until his death in 1961, Hemingway never got around to settling on a title for his moving memoir of his life as a struggling writer in Paris in the 1920s. Over the years he toyed with titles as disparate as *The Eye and the Ear,*

To Write It Truly, Love Is Hunger, It Is Different in the Ring, and *The Parts Nobody Knows*. Posthumously published, *A Moveable Feast* was given its title by Hemingway's widow, Mary, who found inspiration in a letter Hemingway wrote to a friend in 1950: "If you are lucky enough to have lived in Paris as a young man, then wherever you go for the rest of your life, it stays with you, for Paris is a moveable feast."

∽

O. HENRY
Cabbages and Kings (1904)

O. HENRY, whose real name was William Sydney Porter, worked as a clerk, a bank teller in Texas, and a journalist (he founded a magazine called *The Rolling Stone*). During his stint as a teller he was accused of embezzlement, and he fled to Central America, which was the scene of his nineteen linked stories *Cabbages and Kings*. Henry chose his title because he liked the way Lewis Carroll's Walrus "talked of many things" ("The Walrus and the Carpenter," in *Through the Looking-Glass*). Henry's stories described the many improbable and incongruous facets of life in an eccentric Central American country he called Coralio.

> "The time has come," the Walrus said,
> "To talk of many things:
>   Of shoes—and ships—and sealing-wax—
> Of cabbages—and kings—
>   And why the sea is boiling hot—
> And whether pigs have wings."

⏤⏥

PETER HOEG
Smilla's Sense of Snow (1993)

A SPELLBINDING tale of terror set amidst the vast snowy
reaches of Arctic Greenland, *Smilla's Sense of Snow* fea-
tures a thirty-seven-year-old part-Inuit investigator (Smilla
Qaavigaaq Jaspersen) who stumbles into a sinister tangle of
corporate greed and murder and barely escapes with her
life. An unexpected best-seller, it was compared to the best
of Le Carré and to the movie *Alien*, won rave reviews, and
was the object of a heated (and expensive) auction for the
paperback rights.

Danish author Hoeg had published a number of books
before this, but *Smilla's Sense of Snow* was his first to be
translated into English. It was originally called *A Sense of
Snow*, but his American publisher worried that such a subtly
titled book by a largely unknown (to the American public)
writer might suffer in today's highly competitive market.
Toying with possibilities, they suggested Anglicizing
Hoeg's name to Peter Hawk, which might make him seem
more like a brand-name thriller writer. When the author
heard of this idea, he responded in kind, and insisted not
only on keeping his Danish name but on putting his
courageous heroine's name right up front in the title.
Despite protests from interested parties (book clubs, paperback reprinters) in the book community, the addition of
such an unusual name as Smilla into Hoeg's title may have
made the novel even more of a literary event.

Smilla's Sense of Snow is now instantly recognizable and

memorable; by acceding to its author's request the American publisher now has on its list a uniquely titled book that will certainly be in print for many years.

❦

ALDOUS HUXLEY
Brave New World (1932)

A nightmarish vision of a future world in which scientific research clashes with individual liberties (with bad results for liberties), Huxley's novel presents a very pessimistic view of man's progress. Shakespeare's tale of a lonely island inhabited by a witch and a misshaped monster gave Huxley his title.

> MIRANDA: O wonder!
>   How many goodly creatures are there here!
>   How beauteous mankind is! O brave new world
>   That has such people in't!
> PROSPERO: 'Tis new to thee.
> —*The Tempest,* Act V

❦

According to his first wife, Jean Stafford, the Pulitzer Prize–winning poet Robert Lowell revised his work so extensively before being satisfied with it that a poem he began with the title "To Jean: On Her Confirmation" ended up being called "To a Whore at the Brooklyn Navy Yard."

⌒

WILLIAM INGE
Splendor in the Grass (1961)

*M*IDWESTERN dramatist Inge was the author of *Picnic,
Come Back, Little Sheba, Bus Stop,* and other Broadway
hits. His 1961 play was set in a small town in Kansas, and
told of the young love of Deanie and Bud. The loss of
youth and innocence was a steady theme in Inge's dramas,
as were loneliness and disappointment. (Despite his suc-
cesses Inge eventually killed himself.) Thus Wordsworth's
poem "Intimations of Immortality from Recollections of
Early Childhood" gave Inge a bittersweet note:

> Though nothing can bring back the hour
> Of splendor in the grass, of glory in the flower.

⌒

All pieces should be called by the best of *New Yorker*
titles, [Irwin Shaw's] "The Girls in Their Summer
Dresses."   JAMES THURBER

⌒

CHRISTOPHER ISHERWOOD
The Berlin Stories (1939)

*B*RITISH expatriate Isherwood spent five years in Berlin,
from 1929 to 1933, and witnessed both the end of
a singularly decadent society and the rise of the most

authoritarian government ever known. His semi-fictional chronicle of those mad, happy days was first called *The Lost,* evoking the passing of democracy in Germany as well as the underside of life his mostly nocturnal characters, such as the immortal Sally Bowles, inhabit. Isherwood delighted in the "wonderfully ominous" sound of his title. But as his linked stories grew more jumbled and merry and as Nazi Germany grew more vicious and intolerant, *The Lost* seemed too pointed. Isherwood named his tales instead *Mr. Norris Changes Trains.* (His American publisher, though, found the image of changing trains "too obscure" for a potentially saleable book, and insisted on the more dramatic *The Last of Mr. Norris,* which Isherwood reluctantly accepted.) Eventually Isherwood published all of his Berlin-related tales under the blanket title *Berlin Tales,* which he later adapted for the stage under the title *I Am a Camera,* after a line of the narrator's dialogue. And for the stories' Broadway and Oscar-winning movie incarnations they became *Cabaret,* which is, incorrectly, how the book is best known.

⌒

JAMES JONES
From Here to Eternity (1951)

*F*OR his first novel, which was one of the last books edited by the legendary Maxwell Perkins, Jones had considered several titles he found appropriate to his theme of life on a corrupt military base: *Old Soldiers Never Die, If Wishes Were Horses,* and *They Merely Fade Away.* A song in the repertory of Yale's Whiffenpoofs caught his attention, and he settled on it when he learned it came from Rudyard Kipling's "Gentlemen Rankers":

We're poor little lambs who've lost our way,
   Baa! Baa! Baa!
We're little black sheep who've gone astray,
   Baa—aa—aa!
Gentlemen rankers out on the spree,
Damned from here to Eternity,
God ha' mercy on such as we,
   Baa! Yah! Baa!

A woman who (as one did in the Scribner Bookstore) wanders among the counters, saying: "I want a book for a man thirty-four or thirty-five"; will make her choice from those the salesman spreads before her by title. She will glance at the picture on the wrap, read the blurb, look, perhaps, for the publisher's name as one might look for 'Schenley' or 'Hiram Walker' on the label of an unfamiliar bottle and buy the book because the title has provoked her.

ROGER BURLINGAME

JAMES JOYCE
Finnegans Wake (1939)

JAMES Joyce's circular story about Humphrey Chimpden Earwicker, told almost entirely in multilingual puns, sometimes stumped even its creator. When asked by friends what he could possibly call it, Joyce responded that he was

at a loss. "It is like a mountain that I tunnel into from every direction, but I don't know what I will find." Eventually he settled on a name that, naturally, included several allusions to Irish matters. One recalled the famous Irish ballad of Tim Finnegan, a hod-carrier who seems to die after falling off a ladder, but who miraculously revives upon smelling whiskey. Joyce also evoked the legendary Irish seer Finn MacCumhal and Finn's vision of Irish history. Joyce came to love his chosen title. Keeping it secret as he worked on the book, he often challenged his friends to guess it from the text, offering 1000 francs to anyone who could come up with *Finnegans Wake*. "The title is very simple and as commonplace as could be," he taunted, hinting at the many puns he could make from his two words.

NUMBERS IN TITLES

The Taking of Pelham One Two Three

Ball Four

Five Children and It

Six Degrees of Separation

Seventh Heaven

Eight Men Out

The Nine Tailors

Ten Little Indians

Eleven Harrowhouse

Cheaper by the Dozen

The Thirteen Clocks

⌁

BEL KAUFMAN
Up the Down Staircase (1964)

*K*AUFMAN fondly calls her hilarious look at a teacher's
life "the staircase that never seems to rust." The book's
genesis was a three-page story published in the *Saturday
Review* as "From a Teacher's Wastebasket." A book editor at
McGraw-Hill, Gladys Carr, read the story and asked Kaufman to expand it into a novel, using the same collage
technique as in her story. Kaufman tried out several titles,
including *Hi, Teach!, Please Do Not Erase, The Paper World of
Sylvia Barrett*, and *And Gladly Teche*. One of the McGraw-Hill
editors suggested *Don't Shoot Until You See the Pupils*, which
Kaufman thankfully ignored. At last she found her title in
the manuscript itself, as a note sent by the Admiral Ass
(Administrative Assistant) to the teacher with a delinquent
boy: "Detained by me for going up the down staircase
and subsequent insolence." The phrase has entered the
language—and not just the English language, but all over
the world—as the title of newspaper and magazine articles,
as cartoons, and even in the former Soviet newspaper *Pravda*
to illustrate a political drawing.

⌁

D. H. Lawrence's great book titles came only after a
struggle; all his original titles were eventually
changed. *Paul Morel* became *Sons and Lovers*, *John
Thomas and Lady Jane* became *Lady Chatterley's Lover*,

> *The Sisters* became *The Rainbow,* and *The Wedding Ring*
> became *Women in Love.*

❧

SINCLAIR LEWIS
Main Street (1920)

*N*OBEL Prize winner Lewis stirred up a firestorm when
he published his novel about small-town America,
Main Street. Challenging the cherished notion of village life
in rural America as honest "Christian" living, Lewis exposed
its hypocrisy and intolerance. The result was a wave of hate
mail and hostile sermons preached throughout the country.
Lewis had planned to call his book *The Village Virus,* a less
subtle thrust. (Not known for the beauty of his titles, he
was also at this time working on a play to be called *President
Poodle.*) Ironically, for many readers "Main Street" has come
to evoke not the monotony and boredom of small-town life
as Lewis intended, but a rosy, idealized version of life, a
happy, paradisical alternative to life in the big city.

❧

SINCLAIR LEWIS
Babbitt (1922)

Babbitt: a business or professional man who conforms
unthinkingly to prevailing middle-class standards.
—*Merriam Webster's Collegiate Dictionary*

*L*EWIS's savagely funny portrait of the ultimate conform-
ist not only has stayed continuously in print since it
was published but gave America a vivid new word. Would

the word have lasted as long had Lewis used his original idea for his protagonist's name: *Pumphrey*? "In America," Lewis wrote as he worked over the manuscript of what was later to be rechristened *Babbitt*, "we have created the superman complete, and the mellifluous name of the archangelic monster is Pumphrey, good old G. T. Pumphrey, the plain citizen and omnipotent power." And he was to live in Monarch City, not Zenith, his notes reveal, as "the ruler of America, the Tired Businessman, the man with toothbrush mustache and harsh voice who talks about motors and prohibition in the smoking compartment of the Pullman car, the man who plays third-rate golf and first-rate poker at a second-rate country club near an energetic American city."

⁊

Before settling on *Marching On*, James Boyd, author of the 1925 best-seller *Drums*, tried out titles that unbeknownst to him would become classics in the future, including *The Prisoner, Deliverance,* and *The Grapes of Wrath*.

⁊

LARRY McMURTRY
Horseman, Pass By (1961)

*T*HE title of Texas novelist McMurtry's wrenching first novel, which was later made into the movie *Hud*, comes from "Under Ben Bulben" by William Butler Yeats (these lines are also carved into Yeats's tombstone):

Cast a cold eye
On life, on death.
Horseman, pass by!

&

As I was writing the poem "Eighteen Days without You"—the last poem in *Love Poems*—my husband said to me, "I can't stand it any longer, you haven't been with me for days." That poem originally was "Twenty-One Days without You" and it became "Eighteen Days" because he had cut into the inspiration; he demanded my presence back again, into his life, and I couldn't take that much from him.   ANNE SEXTON

&

SOMERSET MAUGHAM
The Moon and Sixpence (1919)

*M*AUGHAM was very proud of his book titles and went out of his way to bring them up in conversation, often adding, "A good title is the title of a book that's successful." Once Maugham was playing bridge with a young friend who said that he found *The Moon and Sixpence* a very good title. "Do you know what it means?" asked Maugham. "People tell me it's a good title but they don't know what it means. It means reaching for the moon and missing the sixpence at one's feet."

❧

SOMERSET MAUGHAM
Of Human Bondage (1915)

*T*HE novel that made Maugham famous was discovered by a young would-be writer who was struggling to earn a living as a manuscript reader at a publishing house—Sinclair Lewis. Maugham's first choice for a title was from Isaiah: *Beauty and Ashes*, which as an image seemed to epitomize the tragedy of the character Philip Carey. It was already taken as a title, though, so Maugham changed it to *Of Human Bondage*, one of the books in Spinoza's *Ethics*.

❧

SOMERSET MAUGHAM
The Razor's Edge (1944)

*M*AUGHAM's use of an ancient Hindu text, the *Katha Upanishad*, to entitle his last great novel is not surprising, as the book is set largely in India. Maugham's hero Larry Darrell's search for meaning in his life leads him to value the spiritual over the material. The Sanskrit *Upanishads* provide good commentary: "The sharp edge of a razor is difficult to pass over; thus the wise say the path to Salvation is hard."

❧

The Psychology of Spiritual Growth had a certain appeal as a book title, if somewhat scholarly. When the publisher asked for something a little, well, flashier, the author came up with a title that has, as of this writing, stayed on the best-seller list for over ten years: *The Road Less Traveled*, by M. Scott Peck.

COLORS IN BOOK TITLES

The Red Badge of Courage

A Clockwork Orange

How Green Was My Valley

A Yellow Raft in Blue Water

Black Like Me

Dress Gray

White Noise

Forever Amber

HERMAN MELVILLE
Moby-Dick (1851)

*M*ELVILLE worked for years on his mighty sea epic, which he always called, very literally, *The Whale*. And despite the profusion of exotic names he invented for his characters, such as Ahab or Queequeg, *The Whale* is how he thought of his great white monster. "Shall I send you a fin of *The Whale*," Melville wrote to his friend Nathaniel Hawthorne, offering to let him read the work-in-progress, "by way of a specimen mouthful? The tail is not yet cooked—though the hell-fire in which the whole book is

boiled might not unreasonably have cooked it all ere this."
In England, Melville's publisher, who had originally rejected
The Whale as not good enough to be a children's book,
finally offered it to the public as juvenile fiction. Harper
and Brothers in New York felt differently, and having read
a real-life newspaper account of a monumental chase at sea
involving a mammoth white whale called Mocha Dick,
suggested that Melville play up on the public's awareness of
the news with a very subtle change of name. It didn't
work—the book was one of the greatest publishing failures
of its time—but who today has not heard of the mighty
Moby-Dick?

During an interview Ann Beattie admitted that she
often can't come up with a title for her stories, so she
submits them untitled. At *The New Yorker* her editor,
Roger Angell, who is himself a distinguished writer,
titles stories he rejects. Letters come back to Beattie's
agent saying, "We are returning X . . . ," and the title
is almost always perfect, says Beattie.

Three surefire best-sellers I would like to write are:
*How to Make Love and Money, How to Tell Your Blessings
from Your Burdens,* and *How to Pass the Joneses at a Dogtrot.*
JAMES THURBER

⊙

Margaret Mitchell
Gone with the Wind (1936)

*T*HERE are several potential sources for what has become one of the most famous book titles in modern fiction. For some ten years this massive novel of the American Civil War was composed under the working title of *Pansy*, which was what Georgia native Mitchell had originally christened the heroine we know as Scarlett O'Hara. Even after the Macmillan Company had taken on the book and was within six months of publishing it, *Pansy* was how it was planned to go out into the world. At the last moment, though, Mitchell wavered, and changed it to *Tote the Weary Load* (after a song the now-named Scarlett had once sung with Rhett Butler—"Just a few more days for to tote the weary load," from Stephen Foster's "Old Kentucky Home"). Then she suggested *Tomorrow Is Another Day*, after Scarlett's famous envoi, but dropped it when she discovered that sixteen other books in print began with the word "tomorrow." Finally she fell back on a phrase she had used at a critical moment in the book, as Scarlett returns to her beloved Tara from Atlanta: "Was Tara still standing? Or was Tara also gone with the wind which had swept through Georgia?" The phrase itself came from a line in a poem by Ernest Dowson called "Non sum qualis eram bonae sub regno Cynarae" ("I am not what I was under the rule of the kind Cynara"). The third stanza begins, "I have forgot much, Cynara! gone with the wind,/ flung roses, roses riotously with the throng." Mitchell loved the romantic imagery: "It could either refer to times that are gone with the snows of yesteryear, to the things that passed with the wind of the war or to a person who went with a wind rather than standing against it." It is said that Mitchell also considered the titles *Jettison*, *Milestones*, and *Ba! Ba! Black Sheep*.

Sometimes, mistaken titles have their own comic appropriateness. Elaine Steinbeck, John Steinbeck's widow, remembers asking in a Yokohama bookstore whether they carried her husband's novel *The Grapes of Wrath*. After checking, the clerk replied that they indeed did carry the book *Angry Raisins*. Flannery O'Connor was informed by Texas friends of a bookstore clerk who mangled the title of *The Violent Bear It Away* into *The Bear that Ran Away with It*. And the publisher of the book you are reading once received a bookstore order for Ortega y Gasset's critique of mass man and mass culture that requested *The Revolt of Them Asses*.

Mother Goose Rhymes (1719)

*T*HERE really was a Mother Goose; she was the mother-in-law of an eighteenth-century Boston printer. Elizabeth Foster married Isaac Goose, who had ten children from a previous marriage, to which were added six more from this union. To keep all her children occupied, Mrs.— now known as "Mother"—Goose made up rhymes, songs,

and tales which she repeated endlessly, so much so that her son-in-law is said to have been "almost driven distracted." He printed up her stories under the title *Songs for the Nursery, or Mother Goose's Melodies for Children,* a collection still read almost three hundred years later.

**HARRY KEMELMAN'S
BELOVED RABBI SMALL
SERIES:**

Monday the Rabbi Took Off
Tuesday the Rabbi Saw Red
Wednesday the Rabbi Got Wet
Thursday the Rabbi Walked Out
Friday the Rabbi Slept Late
Saturday the Rabbi Went Hungry
Sunday the Rabbi Stayed Home
Someday the Rabbi Will Leave
The Day the Rabbi Resigned

≈

JOHN NICHOLS
The Sterile Cuckoo (1965)

*N*ICHOLS's first published novel was christened with its now-famous title from the very beginning. "I was very conscious of the multiple connotations of the title," Nichols has written. "For starters, of course, 'cuckoo' simply means a person who is a bit nuts, kinda loco, kooky, so that sure fit my main character, Pookie Adams. But also, the book was about a kind of sterility, about a person's inability to go deeper into a relationship, take it seriously, face up to what's entailed, and so that's where 'sterile' came in. Too, I was very conscious of the fact that some cuckoos lay their eggs in other birds' nests and do not take responsibility for their young, but let others raise them. I thought that also applied to Pookie Adams, who in the end was really afraid to pursue her relationship with Jerry: she killed it, she didn't take responsibility for the thing she started. So, all along, I thought it was a nicely ambiguous title."

⤳

JOHN NICHOLS
The Milagro Beanfield War (1974)

*N*ICHOLS always wanted to call the first volume of his projected New Mexico Trilogy *The Milagro Beanfield War*. When it came time to publish the book, though, his agent and his publisher balked. "They felt it was too cumbersome, that you couldn't sell a book with a 'foreign' word in the title. Americans wouldn't understand and would be alienated," Nichols has said. Despite the title's meaning—"milagro" is Spanish for "miracle" and describes the transformation of a down-and-out farming community—it was suggested the title be changed, and the publisher even designed a cover with a new title, *Coyote Angels*, printed in bold. Nichols prevailed, but "of course, the Powers That Be were correct; the title really buffaloed people. It was difficult to say, and to understand. The book went nowhere." Eventually, however, there was a turnaround in feeling, the book started to sell, and a hit movie was made of it. The book and its title are so popular now that the word "milagro" is something of a cliché in the Southwest, applied as it is to bed and breakfasts, galleries, tours, and even an organic gardening company. Such are the wages of success.

❧

Thomas Berger, author of *Little Big Man* and *Neighbors*, among many other novels, has said that his source of titles is "the same never-never land from which my characters emigrate without warning."

❧

EDWIN O'CONNOR
The Last Hurrah (1956)

"*I* wanted to do a novel on the whole Irish-American business," O'Connor told a reporter once. "What the Irish got in America, they got through politics; so, of course, I had to use a political framework." And so *Not Moisten an Eye* was begun. O'Connor's magnificent tale of big-city mayor Frank Skeffington's last political campaign won a Pulitzer Prize, but only after O'Connor's editors changed its title, thought to be just a little too Irish in sentiment for the general public, to *The Last Hurrah*.

❧

In an interesting twist on the title game, Donald Trump's paperback publishers found themselves with a problem on their hands when it came time to issue the newly bankrupted businessman's second book, *Surviving at the Top*. While his first book, *The Art of the Deal*, had been a huge bestseller, times had changed for Trump, and not for the better, as he found himself on an allowance doled out monthly by his creditors and the banks. With some nimble footwork the paperback house changed Trump's title to *The Art of Survival*, thus assuring the survival of the book in a tough marketplace.

⌒

JOHN O'HARA
Appointment in Samarra (1934)

O'HARA's first novel, a tragic account of a young man's inability to escape the rigid confines of his middle-class life, was written late at night in a hotel room in New York City. The young writer, who was subsidized by his eager publisher, would spend his days at the movies, in saloons, or socializing with his friends, and got down to his manuscript only after the midnight hour. *The Infernal Grove*, as his novel was then called, was nearly completed when one day O'Hara was having tea with Dorothy Parker. Parker handed O'Hara a copy of a Somerset Maugham play that was currectly on stage, *Sheppey*, to show him a particularly interesting part involving an ancient legend set in Samarra. It seemed that one day a servant returned frightened from the marketplace in Baghdad, telling his master he'd just been jostled by Death. Begging his master

for a horse, the servant then fled to the city of Samarra, where Death would not find him. Shortly thereafter the master ran into Death at the marketplace and asked him why he'd startled his servant. Death replied that it was he who had been startled, not expecting to see the servant in Baghdad; Death had an appointment with him that very evening in Samarra. Reading Maugham's text, O'Hara exclaimed that he had found the perfect title for his book: *Appointment in Samarra.* It echoed perfectly the efforts of O'Hara's hero to fight—unsuccessfully—his own fate. "Oh, I don't think so, Mr. O'Hara. Do you?" Parker replied. "Dorothy didn't like the title," noted O'Hara. "Alfred Harcourt [O'Hara's publisher] didn't like the title, his editors didn't like it, nobody liked it but me. But I bulled it through."

∽

JOHN O'HARA
Butterfield 8 (1935)

*I*N the 1930s the New York Telephone Company announced that a distinguishing numeral was to be placed with the name of each central telephone office. Patrons were to dial the first two letters of the named area of New York plus an added number, RHinelander 4, for instance. BUtterfield 8 was the phone exchange for the middle of the monied Upper East Side, the neighborhood where many of protagonist Gloria Wandrous's activities take place, and so symbolized her short and decadent life.

⌐

> Ordinarily I do not bother to explain the names I give
> my books. After a book has been in print a few
> months people stop trying to figure out what, if any,
> significance the title has; and no matter how right a
> title may be in the English language editions, it
> probably will be changed for the translations. *But-*
> *terfield* 8, in the French translation, became *Gloria*,
> about as uninspired a mutation as an author could
> hope to avoid. JOHN O'HARA

⌐

JOHN O'HARA
A Rage to Live (1949)

*I*N a letter to his editor, the famed Saxe Commins,
O'Hara had the following to say about this title, and
book titles in general: "The best thing about it, or one of
the best, is the unusual juxtaposition of simple words. The
best thing about it is how it, and the whole poem from
which it comes [Alexander Pope's *Moral Essays*], apply to
my novel. And another thing about it is that I like it.
Actually, although my titles are usually pretty good, people
don't buy books by titles as much as they do by the author's
name. I know I do."

❧

Every one of my novels could be entitled *The Unbear-
able Lightness of Being* or *The Joke* or *Laughable Loves*;
the titles are interchangeable, they reflect the small
number of themes that obsess me, define me, and,
unfortunately, restrict me. Beyond these themes, I
have nothing else to say or write.   MILAN KUNDERA

❧

EUGENE O'NEILL
Mourning Becomes Electra (1931)

*P*LAYWRIGHT O'Neill had been unhappy with Horace
Liveright, his publisher, and managed to get rival
editor Saxe Commins interested in his work. Commins later
noted what had happened when the first O'Neill play to be
delivered to Harper and Brothers was examined: "There was
general dismay over the title. The then editor-in-chief
looked at the sheaf of papers, concentrated on the title
page, played for a while with the long black ribbon on his
spectacles, cleared his throat as a preliminary to uttering a
shattering profundity, shook his white-thatched head and
exploded the word 'meaningless' with an implied exclama-
tion mark at the end of it. As on cue, the editorial assistants
and the publicity director embellished the verdict with
even stronger adjectives, both commercial and semantic.
. . . They insisted, as publishers habitually do, that a book
title must smite the beholder in the eye, whether it applies

91

to the contents or not, and must, above all, be easily remembered." A play about a Civil War—era New England family, its title uses "becomes" as in "flatters." O'Neill echoes the ancient Greek story of Agamemnon's daughter Electra who is surrounded by death and is thus accustomed to mourning.

᠎

George Plimpton has recounted how, as a schoolboy, he spent many hours randomly jotting down ideas for book titles to amuse himself. Once he began writing books, however, he couldn't come up with titles at all. Plimpton's most famous book—about playing as an amateur on a professional football team—went to its publisher untitled. With one day to go Plimpton was still without inspiration, until his publisher called to suggest *Where Are You, Dink Stover?*, after a much earlier series of boys' books by Owen Johnson (*Stover at Lawrenceville, Stover at Yale,* etc.). Plimpton credits "divine guidance" for *Paper Lion,* which his pencil formed as if by magic on a sheet of paper. He called his publisher. " 'Buz, I've got it!' and I told him. After quite a pause he said, 'You mean you don't like *Where Are You, Dink Stover?'* "

Ex Libris

⁂

GEORGE ORWELL
1984 (1949)

*N*OVELIST Orwell began his frightening portrayal of life in a future totalitarian state in 1943, when World War II had entered its darkest hours. He didn't complete it until after the Allied victory; but even with the war's conclusion the world was still facing grave dangers. The Cold War had begun in earnest. Physically and morally Europe was in a shambles, and Orwell's choice for a title for his grim vision reflected that despair: *The Last Man in Europe*. It seemed too bleak, though, and in an effort to postpone the reality of his fictional world he decided to call it *1984*, which was both far enough away to seem unlikely and a simple reversal of numbers of the year in which he finished writing his book.

⁂

EDGAR ALLAN POE
"The Bells" (1849)

*I*N the spring of 1848 an emotionally exhausted Poe went to visit his friend Mrs. Marie Shew in lower New York City, hoping for enough quiet and rest to be able to write a new poem for publication. He found the opposite, as Mrs. Shew's house rang with the sounds of many neighboring churches' bells throughout the day. Poe, who admitted to "no feeling, no sentiment, no inspiration," could think of little else besides the bells. Accordingly, one day after tea, Mrs. Shew took out a piece of paper and wrote across the top, "The Bells, by E. A. Poe," to which she added, "the little silver bells." Poe made little headway into the poem, so Mrs. Shew wrote on another sheet "the heavy iron bells." At first Poe wryly referred to it as "Mrs. Shew's poem," but soon he found his inspiration and completed, on his own, one of his most powerful and melodious poems.

❧

Like *Babbitt*, *Pollyanna* has found its way into the dictionary as a word. Taken from the title of Eleanor Holmes's 1913 novel, a Pollyanna is described in *Webster's* as "a person characterized by irrepressible optimism and a tendency to find good in everything."

❧

KATHERINE ANNE PORTER
Ship of Fools (1962)

*I*N 1931 Texas-born novelist and short story writer Porter traveled from Mexico to Europe on the German ship S.S. *Werra*. The trip, during which she observed the wretchedness and hopes of a most unusual assortment of fellow passengers, made a vivid impression. Almost immediately Porter began writing about it in a series of short stories she called *Promised Land*, and later, as the tragedy of the Nazi regime loomed, *No Safe Harbor*. Upon completing her manuscript, which she had worked into a complete novel, she was inspired by the title *Ship of Fools*. It came from *Das Narrenschiff* ("ship of fools"), a moral allegory written at the turn of the sixteenth century which Porter had read right after her sea voyage. As Porter noted, "I took for my own this simple, almost universal image of the ship of this world on its voyage to eternity. It is by no means new—it was very old and durable and dearly familiar when Brant [author of *Das Narrenschiff*] used it; and it suits my purpose exactly. I am a passenger on that ship." Porter held firm when friends suggested the title might indicate to readers that Porter was contemptuous of her fictional characters and, by extension, of humanity.

⇌

CHARLES PORTIS
True Grit (1968)

*W*HEN he began writing his great Western adventure, Portis had no particular title in mind. "There was no title," he remembered. "Early on I had used the expression in a line of dialogue, and then, a little further along, it occurred to me that it might do for a title. I went back and wrote it on the first page of the typescript and there it stayed. At that time I was reading books about the Southern frontier, mostly memoirs, in which all the most admired people had something called 'grit'—meaning they were steadfast, determined. It could suggest too a kind of cranky obstinacy. I had never seen it in such profusion as in these books. There was grit, plain grit, plain old grit, clear grit, pure grit, pure dee grit (a euphemism for damned) and true grit. Thus the hard little word was in my head when I began the story." Portis has pointed out that, oddly enough, the phrase "true grit" turns up in Bram Stoker's 1897 novel *Dracula*, describing one of the characters!

~

THOMAS PYNCHON
V. (1963)

*I*T has been suggested that Thomas Pynchon is an alias used by one or another of several quite famous writers who want to experiment with fiction different from what they are already known for writing. Some say Pynchon is really the front name for an exceptionally gifted but otherwise anonymous editor (this is probably an editor's idea). Others say Pynchon died some time ago, or never existed. Whatever Pynchon's story might be, his first novel, which was submitted to a publisher as *Low Lands*, came to have as many working titles as the author has been attributed identities. The young editor at Lippincott, Corlies Smith, who acquired *Low Lands* suggested calling it *The Quest of Herbert Stencil* or *The Yo-Yo World of Benny Profane* or *World on a String*, which latter title Pynchon more or less liked, admitting that he himself was terrible with book titles. Pynchon then countered with his own new idea: *Blood's a Rover*, after a line from a poem by A. E. Housman. On being told that that phrase conjured up images of Mickey Spillane or even Sabatini, Pynchon tried *Down Paradise Street*, *Of a Fond Ghoul*, *Footsteps of the Gone*, *Dream Tonight of Peacock Tails*, and *The Republican Party Is a Machine* (all of these titles have a source both in the book *V.* and in the public domain— the reader can try to find them). The game spun out of

control, and a return to the simple *V.*, the name of the not-so-simple mysterious presence in the novel, solved the dilemma.

❧

> The title [*Of the Farm*] originally was simply *The Farm*, but this had a monumentality that seemed bogus to me, which the preposition "Of" suitably reduced; I intended to mean that the book was *about* the farm, and that the people in it belonged *to* the farm, were of the earth, earthy, mortal, fallen, and imperfect.
>
> JOHN UPDIKE

❧

J. D. SALINGER
The Catcher in the Rye (1951)

THE Catcher in the Rye has been highly controversial since it was first published. It has been banned from school libraries, analyzed for its supposed hidden meaning, and even burned. Its title remains as enigmatic as ever, but it comes from a passage in the novel when its hero, Holden Caulfield, is asked by his sister to name something he would like to be. Holden imagines himself as a shepherd of sorts, protecting small children. Standing in a field of rye, he watches them as they play happily about him. "I have to catch everybody if they start to go over the cliff," says Holden. "I'd just be the catcher in the rye and all. I know it's crazy, but that's the only thing I'd really like to be."

Salinger has never commented on the book since its publication, and has become as well known for his reclusiveness as for his writing. In 1951, Harry Scherman, the founder of the Book-of-the-Month Club, which had selected the book as a Main Selection, asked Salinger if he would consider changing the title to something less peculiar. After a moment of thought Salinger replied, "Holden Caulfield wouldn't like that."

❧

ROBERT SHERWOOD
The Petrified Forest (1935)

FORMER *Life* magazine editor Sherwood, who had won a Pulitzer Prize for his play *Idiot's Delight*, started writing dialogue for a new play without much idea of where it was headed. He had just moved into a new office, which was bare except for a lone and incongruous road map. Leafing through it Sherwood decided to set his play, which he had decided would be about a group of gangsters who take over a local diner, in a town out in the Arizona desert. In the first act the diner's waitress asks where a customer, a drifter passing through, is headed, and the man replies that it all depends on where the road goes. When Sherwood looked more closely at his map, the road from his imagined diner in fact led to the Petrified Forest, and in that instant Sherwood knew how his play would unfold and what its title had to be.

꒰

Short story collections are the hardest things on earth
to name—to get a title which is at once arresting,
inviting, applicable and inclusive and doesn't sound
like a rehash of the titles of O. Henry, or isn't an
aenemic Namby Pamby wishy-washy phrase.

F. SCOTT FITZGERALD

꒰

WILLIAM L. SHIRER
The Rise and Fall of the Third Reich (1960)

*I*N 1949 William L. Shirer, who had had a distinguished
career as a foreign correspondent and broadcaster in
Europe and Asia, was finishing a novel at his editor's house.
When asked if he knew what he was going to write next,
Shirer replied, "For once in my life I not only know what I
am going to write; I even know the title. It's going to be
called *The Rise and Fall of the Third Reich*." His editor
responded, "Bill, please God, don't ask us to publish a book
called *The Rise and Fall of the Third Reich*." So Shirer began
looking around for a new publisher, without much luck.
Finally, an editor at Simon & Schuster decided to take a
chance on it, and paid Shirer an advance of $10,000. "As it
turned out," remembered Shirer, "that was $10,000 for ten
years of work . . ." After ten years of research he was broke.
"And I expected to stay broke," Shirer recalled. "Simon &
Schuster said their salesmen didn't think they could sell the

book, and the first print order was quite small. One of the editors told me, 'You'd better think of making your money somewhere else.' "

The book has since become one of the best-selling books of all time in both hardcover and paperback and has been translated into almost every language in the world.

➔

In the early years of this century there was a well-known bookman's gag based upon the notion that the ideal book title would combine topics known to be best-selling ones and, at that time, the proposal was for *Lincoln's Doctor's Dog.* Much later a Simon & Schuster editor came up with one that better suited the smash hits of his day, even though it didn't include *How to,* namely, *A Treasury of Filthy Religious Art Masterpieces.*   PETER SCHWED

➔

GERTRUDE STEIN
The Autobiography of Alice B. Toklas (1933)

*W*HILE she did write the famous *Alice B. Toklas Cookbook,* about dazzling meals with the famous painters and writers who made France synonymous with culture and beauty—and which included the notorious hashish brownies recipe—Alice Toklas never wrote her *Autobiography.* Her expatriate companion Gertrude Stein, who could never be persuaded to write her own autobiography, did Alice's instead in one short six-week stretch. *My Life with the Great,*

Stein teasingly called it, and *My Twenty-Five Years with Gertrude Stein* and, best of all, *Wives of Geniuses I Have Sat With.* The result made the shy, nearly-invisible-by-choice Toklas a literary celebrity, much to Stein's amusement. "Alice B. Toklas did hers," she said, "and now anybody will do theirs. . . . Autobiography is easy like it or not autobiography is easy for any one."

One of Gertrude Stein's most evocative poem titles, "Before the Flowers of Friendship Faded Friendship Faded," came from her lifelong companion Alice B. Toklas, who claimed to have heard a woman in a restaurant say it in French to her luncheon date.

⤳

JOHN STEINBECK
East of Eden (1952)

$\mathcal{B}$ Y the time he was just a few chapters into his great novel of love, sin, and murder, it was clear to Steinbeck that his tale was biblical in nature, scope, and language. Centering on the lives of Adam Trask and his sons Cal and Aron, the tale was too powerful to be called just *The Salinas Valley*, after the lush virgin California landscape that provided its setting. Steinbeck tried to personalize it to *My Valley*, but both author and editor felt that was too weak. It was Steinbeck's wife Elaine who found in Genesis the perfect name, "soft" sounding at first (to Steinbeck) but tough and evocative once one realizes its source. "The title comes from the 16th verse," he wrote a friend, "but the whole passage is applicable."

> Cain said to his brother Abel, "Let us go out in the field." And when they were in the field, Cain rose up against his brother Abel, and killed him. Then the LORD said to Cain, "Where is your brother Abel?" He said, "I do not know; am I my brother's keeper?" And the LORD said, "What have you done? Listen; your brother's blood is crying out to me from the ground. And now you are cursed from the ground, which has opened its mouth to receive your brother's blood from your hand. When you till the ground, it will no longer yield to you its strength; you will be a fugitive and a wanderer on the earth." Cain said to

the LORD, "My punishment is greater than I can bear. Today you have driven me away from the soil, and I shall be hidden from your face; I shall be a fugitive and a wanderer on the earth, and anyone who meets me may kill me." Then the LORD said to him, "Not so. Whoever kills Cain will suffer a sevenfold vengeance." And the LORD put a mark on Cain, so that no one who came upon him would kill him. Then Cain went away from the presence of the LORD, and settled in the land of Nod, east of Eden.

JOHN STEINBECK
The Grapes of Wrath (1939)

*W*ORKING on his new manuscript in 1938, Steinbeck had great trouble concentrating. The next-door neighbors were hammering day and night—pounding—laying floors and driving Steinbeck into a rage. It was his first wife, Carol, who found the title in Julia Ward Howe's "The Battle Hymn of the Republic":

Mine eyes have seen the glory of the coming of the Lord;
He is trampling out the vintage where the grapes of wrath
   are stored;
He hath loosed the fateful lightning of His terrible swift
   sword;
His truth is marching on.

"Marvellous title. The book has being at last," Steinbeck wrote in his journal. And to his agent he said, "I like it

because it is a march and this book is a kind of march—
because it is in our own revolutionary tradition . . ."

᠍᠍᠍ᔧ

In the only known instance of a book's title predicting
its fate, the first printing of John Steinbeck's *The
Wayward Bus* was destroyed when the truck trans-
porting the books from the bindery crashed in flames.
The truck had been hit by a "wayward" bus that had
been traveling down the wrong side of the road.

ᔧ

JOHN STEINBECK
Of Mice and Men (1937)

*T*HE tragic story of the mentally retarded giant Lennie
and his friend George and what happens to tear them
apart needed a stronger title than the working title *Something
that Happened.* Steinbeck found his inspiration in Robert
Burns's "To a Mouse":

> The best-laid schemes o' mice an' men
> Gang aft a-gley
> An' lea'e us nought but grief an' pain,
> For promised joy.

ROBERT LOUIS STEVENSON
Treasure Island (1883)

SCOTTISH writer Stevenson's first novel was born as an amusement for his son Lloyd. It was called *The Sea-Cook;* Stevenson read chapters aloud to his son every day after writing them, and to illustrate his tale he drew a map in watercolors of a mysterious island. The map was beautifully done and Stevenson, his son, and his publishers all liked it so much they unanimously changed the title of his story to *Treasure Island,* after the drawing.

Asked about the title of her 1974 novel *Celestial Navigation,* Anne Tyler said she's always loved the phrase. "I even had a cat by that name."

꼭

BRAM STOKER
Dracula (1897)

*S*TOKER found the name for his fiendish protagonist, the bloodsucking Count Dracula, and for his Gothic adventure, in the story of a historical character. Vlad Tepes (known for various of his proclivities as Vlad the Impaler) was a nobleman of Wallachia (a region in modern-day Romania) who lived during the fifteenth century. Of particularly savage habits, Vlad was also known as "Dracula," which in Wallachian means "devil." The name was commonly given to anyone particularly known for courage, cruelty, or cunning. Over the course of many armed raids into neighboring territory, Vlad butchered tens of thousands of helpless citizens and was said to be fond of dining alone among the impaled corpses of his victims.

꼭

IRVING STONE
Lust for Life (1934)

*B*OTH the story and the title of Stone's ground-breaking fictional biography of painter Vincent Van Gogh seemed to spring ready-made from the author's mind. *Lust for Life* ignited a craze for Van Gogh's work that continues today. After the book was published, policemen had to be called to the Museum of Modern Art to keep order among the unruly lines of art lovers that formed outside the doors. And along Fifth Avenue the fashionable shops filled their windows with reproductions of Van Gogh's paintings as well as sunflower hats and evening gowns, sportswear, gloves, and dresses in Van Gogh colors.

When Stone returned home to California after his initial publicity tour on the East Coast he received a telegram from a New York manufacturer asking permission to put out a "Lust For Life Negligee." ("Can there be greater heights?" a stunned Stone wondered.)

⁖

> "And what is this jive biz school talk? Just cause you got a title now, it don't make you a book."
>
> JAY McINERNY, *Brightness Falls*

⁖

HARRIET BEECHER STOWE
Uncle Tom's Cabin (1852)

"THE little lady who started the big war," as Lincoln reportedly called Mrs. Stowe, took the title and the basic elements of her vigorous abolitionist novel from a true story. Early in the spring of 1851 Tom Sims, a runaway slave from Savannah, Georgia, was found in Boston and taken into custody by a Southern deputy. Sims, surrounded by three hundred policemen who were protecting the deputy from an enraged crowd of anti-slavery citizens, was forcibly returned to slavery. Harriet Stowe heard of this incident and, roused to a fury at the basic inhumanity of much of the United States, wrote her tale and subtitled it "The Man that Was a Thing." Her editor, a little nervous about the book's reception among readers outside of the North, made her change it to the slightly less inflammatory "Life among the Lowly."

∽

WILLIAM THACKERAY
Vanity Fair (1848)

*A*LTHOUGH his massive tragicomedy of the English social scene had already been accepted for publication by Bradbury and Evans, Thackeray was dissatisfied with calling it *The Novel without a Hero: Pen and Pencil Sketches of English Society*. The title was too long, and too unwieldly, and besides it felt like a novel without a title, not a hero. The author then went to the seaside to tinker with his novel and to rest in solitude. There, on a damp November night, Thackeray "ransacked his brain" for a proper title. Lying awake in bed, in the dark, a line from John Bunyan's *The Pilgrim's Progress* suddenly came to him as if from heaven: "It beareth the name of Vanity Fair, because the town where 'tis kept is lighter than vanity." He jumped out of bed and, lighting a candle, ran around his room three times shouting, *"Vanity Fair, Vanity Fair, Vanity Fair!"*

❧

ERNEST LAWRENCE THAYER
"Casey at the Bat" (1888)

*E*NDLESSLY repeated and declaimed, Thayer's mock-heroic poem first appeared in the *San Francisco Examiner* of June 3, 1888. Thayer took his hero's name from a real baseball player, Daniel Maurice Casey, who while not known as a slugger did play as an outfielder and pitcher for Detroit and Philadelphia. His better-known older brother, Dennis, played as an outfielder for Baltimore and New York. Daniel Casey lived until 1943; because of the lack of copyright laws at the time the poem was first published, neither he nor Ernest Thayer ever made any money at all from one of America's most recited poems.

❧

DYLAN THOMAS
Under Milk Wood (1954)

*T*HE Welsh poet and playwright was never known for his affection for his audience. Typical of his scorn was his play title *Llareggub*, certainly a Welsh-looking and -sounding title until one troubles to read it backwards. Feeling that the joke was childish and, besides, too obscure for American theatergoers, friends persuaded Thomas to change his play's name to the more resonant *Under Milk Wood*.

~

J. R. R. TOLKIEN
The Hobbit (1937)

*O*N a hot summer day Tolkien, who was a professor of Middle English at Oxford University, was sitting at his desk correcting papers on English literature. One of his students hadn't completed his examination, and in the blank space on the page Tolkien wrote, quite at random, "In a hole in the ground there lived a hobbit." He later remembered, "Names always generate a story in my mind: eventually I thought I'd better find out what hobbits were like." Thus was a mythology born. Tolkien noted, "I am in fact a hobbit in all but size. I like gardens, trees and unmechanized farmlands; I smoke a pipe, and like good plain food (unrefrigerated), but detest French cooking; I like, and even dare to wear in these dull days, ornamental waistcoats. I am fond of mushrooms (out of a field); have a very simple sense of humor (which even my appreciative critics find tiresome); I go to bed late and get up late (when possible). I do not travel much."

~

J. R. R. TOLKIEN
The Lord of the Rings (1954–56)

*T*HE Lord of the Rings, Tolkien's continuation of the epic *The Hobbit*, was to be published in three volumes and needed three titles. Tolkien's publisher, Allen & Unwin, felt that although the work was not strictly a trilogy—Tolkien felt strongly that it was not—three volumes appearing under three different titles would garner three sets of reviews, which would generate more sales and might encourage the reader otherwise put off by the sheer size of the work. Tolkien insisted on retaining *The Lord of the Rings* as an overall title, but did come up with *The Fellowship of the Ring* (1954), *The Two Towers* (1955), and *The Return of the King* (1956) (although he preferred *The War of the Ring* for the third volume) for the individual tales to satisfy his publisher.

❧

Charles Norris, brother of editor and novelist Frank Norris, gave his books the most succinct titles possible: *Bread, Salt,* and *Brass*. This directness is matched, perhaps, by titles such as Knut Hamsun's *Hunger*, Isaac Bashevis Singer's *Scum*, Harry Crews's *Car*, and Josephine Hart's *Damage*.

❧

Leo Tolstoy
War and Peace (1864–69)

*T*OLSTOY first conceived of his massive novel as a panorama of Russia in the dark post-Napoleonic days of the 1820s; it was to be called *1825*. As his research progressed, though, he realized that the true center of his story, and the plot device with the most potential for excitement and grand sweep, lay right in the middle of the Napoleonic Wars. Shifting his characters back two decades, he retitled his book *1805*, and as such it began publication in serial form in the magazine *Russian Herald*. Many chapters later, Tolstoy decided to call it *All's Well that Ends Well*—he intended to write in happy endings for all his characters. Prince Andrei was to survive his war wounds; Pierre was to marry his true love; and so on. Eventually, however, as the book grew longer and longer, Tolstoy became more grave about his enterprise. It was to be a solemn account of a monumental chapter in Russian history, and as such required a solemn name. *War and Peace*—the basic elements of so many centuries of Russian life—was determined to be the only suitable heading.

LANDSCAPES IN BOOK TITLES

The Magic Mountain

Desert Solitaire

Lost Horizon

The Old Forest

The Green Hills of Africa

On the Beach

The Jungle Book

Woman in the Dunes

The Onion Field

The Cruel Sea

The Ocean of Story

The Cliff Dwellers

> *The Long Valley*
> *A River Runs through It*

⮑

JOHN KENNEDY TOOLE
A Confederacy of Dunces (1980)

*T*OOLE, a young man from New Orleans, couldn't get his novel published. The comic tale of a man fighting the absurdity of the world was rejected so often that Toole committed suicide in despair. Posthumously published— thanks to the tirelessness of Toole's grieving mother—it won a Pulitzer Prize. Toole's title describes the novel to a tee: "When a true genius appears in the world, you may know him by this sign, that the dunces are all in confederacy against him" (Jonathan Swift, "Thoughts on Various Subjects, Moral and Diverting").

⮑

EUDORA WELTY
A Curtain of Green (1941)

"*I*'M terrible about titles," said the great Southern writer Eudora Welty. "I don't know how to come up with them. They're the one thing in the story I'm really uncertain about." Her difficulty with titles started right off with her first collection of stories, the title of which might well have been different. "No one knew what to call the first book. Everyone was against most of the titles. There was only one they had no opinion about at all—*A Curtain of Green*.

My editor said, 'If we call it *A Curtain of Green,* you'll never need another title. Your second book could be *A Curtain of Black* and the one after that *A Curtain of Blue.* Your final book could just be called *Curtains.'* "

I have always had trouble coming up with a title. My favorite title was *The Choirboys* because it was provocative. People wondered why in hell a book about cops would be so titled. My biggest mistake was *The Blooding.* People have reported that they resisted buying it because they thought it was about slasher murders, when actually the title referred to the massive blood testing that was done during the first use of genetic fingerprinting in a British murder inquiry.   JOSEPH WAMBAUGH

❧

PATRICK WHITE
Voss (1957)

*N*OBEL Prize winner Patrick White was a stickler about his book titles. When the Book-of-the-Month Club, which had selected *Voss* as a Main Selection, complained to him about the title, White replied, "A book grows with its title. If one starts to mess around with the latter afterwards, the whole thing begins to look a bit like a bad Hollywood film. Besides, I have recently remembered how, some years ago, before I had started to go anywhere with my writing, one of my aunts dreamed that I had a big success with 'a book with a funny foreign name.' So that is another very good reason why the title must remain."

❧

Some writers have no problem: their title descends in tongues of flame, it's just a matter of choosing a book. *Paradise Lost—Vanity Fair—War and Peace—A Farewell to Arms—The Waste Land* . . . [A title] should stand on its own nor should it be in French or Latin nor contain words which no one knows how to pronounce like pericope or pangolin.   CYRIL CONNOLLY

❧

> The title comes last. TENNESSEE WILLIAMS

❧

TENNESSEE WILLIAMS
A Streetcar Named Desire (1947)

*W*INNER of a Pulitzer Prize, Williams's savage play epitomizes for many the city of New Orleans. Beginning its life as *The Moth*, and then *Blanche's Chair in the Moon*—honoring the image of the faded Southern belle Blanche DuBois waiting in vain in the moonlight for her weak boyfriend—*Streetcar* spent several years in manuscript as *The Poker Night* before finding its now-classic title. Williams wrote in an essay, "I live near the main street in the Quarter [of New Orleans]. Down this street, running on the same tracks, are two streetcars, one named 'Desire' and the other named 'Cemeteries.' Their indiscourageable progress up and down Royal Street struck me as having some symbolic bearing of a broad nature on the life in the Vieux Carré—and everywhere else, for that matter." It is of no small symbolism that the doomed Blanche's first line in the play is, "They told me to take a streetcar named Desire, then transfer to one called Cemeteries."

꙳

TENNESSEE WILLIAMS
The Rose Tattoo (1950)

*O*RIGINALLY called *The Eclipse of May 29, 1919*, and later *Stornella*, Williams's play about a grief-stricken widow, Serafina Delle Rose, and her husband, Rosario, who has a rose tattoo on his chest, found its many allusions to roses in the playwright's sister Rose. Ill enough to be committed to various mental institutions, Rose was a lifelong worry to her brother; as her madness increased during the period in which he wrote *The Rose Tattoo*, Williams was completely distracted, and the titles he played with all focused on his sister's dilemma: *Novena to a Rose, A Candle to a Rose, A Rose for Our Lady, A Rose from the Hand of Our Lady,* and *Perpetual Novena to a Rose.*

꙳

TENNESSEE WILLIAMS
Cat on a Hot Tin Roof (1955)

*T*HE once-supreme athlete turned alcoholic introvert Brick made his debut in a short story called "Three Players of a Summer Game." Williams, dissatisfied with the tale, turned it into a play of the same name and added, as Brick's sensual wife, Maggie—Maggie the Cat. "My father had a great gift for phrases," Williams remembered. "The title 'Cat on a Hot Tin Roof' comes from him. 'Edwina,' he used to say, 'you're making me as nervous as a cat on a hot tin roof!' "

⌐

"He said he rather thought of giving the book no title at all. 'If a book is good enough in itself . . .' he murmured, waving his cigarette.

"Rothenstein objected that absence of title might be bad for the sale of the book. 'If,' he urged, 'I went into a bookseller's and said simply, "Have you got?" or "Have you a copy of?" how would they know what I wanted?' "   MAX BEERBOHM, "Enoch Soames"

FAMILIES IN TITLES
The Good Mother
Life with Father
Uncle Vanya
Sons and Lovers
The Daughter of Time
The Kitchen God's Wife
Cousin Bette
Travels with My Aunt

✑

SLOAN WILSON
The Man in the Gray Flannel Suit (1955)

*A*N editor at Simon & Schuster was working on a novel called *A Candle at Midnight* by reporter Sloan Wilson, but he wasn't enamored of the title, which he felt didn't really evoke Wilson's fictional world of big business. Over dinner with publisher Richard Simon, Wilson's wife referred to her husband's *Time* and *Life* colleagues as "all those men in gray flannel suits." Simon liked the phrase and immediately saw the possibilities for the book's jacket. Pointing to the editor, he said, "And I know where we can get a model—free." Over the editor's protests a suit was bought—in gray flannel, of course—a photo was taken, and *The Man in the Gray Flannel Suit* entered the language.

✑

The Spy Wore Red, Aline, Countess of Romanones's best-selling memoir of life as an American spy during World War II, was originally called *Code Name: Butch*, but the title was changed because *butch* "had other implications," Aline said.

❧

Thomas Wolfe
You Can't Go Home Again (1940)

*P*OSTHUMOUSLY published, Wolfe's last novel contin-
ued the story of George Webber, his autobiographical
hero. Webber's return to his North Carolina hometown
mirrors Wolfe's own return to Asheville after his first novel,
Look Homeward, Angel, was received there with dismay and
vilification. As he was writing his last book Wolfe remi-
nisced with a dinner companion, Ella Winter, widow of
muckraking reporter Lincoln Steffens, telling her of his
humiliating experience. "But don't you know you can't go
home again?" she said. Wolfe leapt on her comment and
now, when the line is uttered, we can think only of
Thomas Wolfe.

❧

The poet Maya Angelou once said that even as a
young woman she never agreed with Thomas Wolfe's
title *You Can't Go Home Again.* Instead, she felt, you
never truly leave your home: "You take it with you;
it's under your fingernails; it's in the hair follicles; it's
in the way you smile; it's in the ride of your hips, in
the passage of your breasts; it's all there, no matter
where you go."

NOW ALL WE NEED IS A TITLE

⌘

THOMAS WOLFE
Look Homeward, Angel (1929)

*W*OLFE's first novel, still considered his best, is thinly disguised autobiography treating the coming of age of a North Carolina boy. Wolfe's title of choice, *O Lost*, made little impression on the sales force of his publisher, Scribner's; they found it flabby, and urged him to try another tack. The garrulous Wolfe, whom some would accuse of overwriting, returned with *The Exile's Story, The Lost Language*, and *They Are Strange and They Are Lost*, among other ideas. His editor, Maxwell Perkins, came to the rescue with a line from Milton's "Lycidas": "Look homeward, Angel, now, and melt with ruth" (that is, have faith in redemption and resurrection).

⌘

It was a dream I had last week
And some kind of record seemed vital.
I knew it wouldn't be much of a poem
But I love the title.
                    WENDY COPE, "Making Cocoa for Kingsley Amis"

⌘

A good experience with a title, or a word or portion of a title, can give rise to further inspirations. The first use of the word "Fireside" [as a title] was when

123

[Simon & Schuster editor] Jack Goodman put together a lovely anthology in the early 1930's entitled *The Fireside Book of Dog Stories*. It sold extremely well and was a Book-of-the-Month Club choice; from then on the word "Fireside" was used almost indiscriminately for an amazing number of variegated gift books. There were Fireside books of love songs and of American songs, a *Fireside Cook Book*, a *Fireside Chess Book*, a *Fireside Treasury of Modern Humor*. A series of Fireside sports books appeared over the years: *Fireside Baseball* (so successful that it was followed by a second and third volume), and Fireside books on boxing, golf, tennis, horse racing, football, fishing—even cards and guns. As a result the name "Fireside" became so identified with Simon & Schuster publishing that when the firm was eager to create substantial lines in the burgeoning quality-paperback market and was looking for names to give identity to the separate divisions, "Fireside" was the choice for one.

PETER SCHWED

❧

TOM WOLFE
Bonfire of the Vanities (1987)

SOCIAL chronicler Wolfe, as well known for his sartorial splendor as for his biting reports on cultural mores, had wanted to use the phrase "bonfire of the vanities" as a book title ever since a trip he'd taken to Florence, Italy. There he toured the Piazza della Signoria, where in the fifteenth century the residents of Florence built a bonfire to burn their worldly goods at the urging of the ascetic monk Savonarola. Florence had sunk into a decadent slough, and the fire was to help cleanse its citizens of sin. Many items went into the fire—books, silver, clothing, paintings—and a second fire was built. After two fires the citizenry had had enough, and a third was constructed to immolate Savonarola himself. The concept of such a bonfire, of immolating one's vanities, attracted Wolfe as a fine idea for a title. Noting that, in fact, his novel of the same name doesn't really reflect the concept of the bonfire, Wolfe was tempted to write an epigraph explaining the reference but felt "I came off as Savonarola . . . it was a far-fetched analogy." Few, if any, critics and readers have ever complained.

❧

In 1938 Winston Churchill published his collected speeches under the title *Arms and the Covenant.* His American publisher felt that an American audience would not be drawn to that title and asked Churchill for an alternative. (For anyone who has ever sat in on an editorial meeting at a publishing house, this story, while perhaps apocryphal, is certainly not improbable.) Churchill wired back, "THE YEARS OF THE LOCUST," which was misread by the cable operator and came through as "THE YEARS OF THE LOTUS." The editors confessed among themselves that while they did not understand Churchill's meaning they would honor the intent. Because the lotus, in Greek legend, was thought to induce sleep, the book was published in America as *While England Slept*, and was hugely successful.

When Simon & Schuster published a children's book called *Dr. Dan the Bandage Man*, they decided as a sales gimmick to include half a dozen adhesive bandages in each book. Publisher Richard Simon had a friend at the Johnson and Johnson Company and sent him a telegram reading, "PLEASE SHIP TWO MILLION BAND-AIDS IMMEDIATELY." The next day he received his reply: "BAND-AIDS ON THEIR WAY. WHAT THE HELL HAPPENED TO YOU?"

"The last volume was written in fourteen days. In this achievement Reardon rose almost to heroic pitch, for he had much to contend with beyond the mere labor of composition. Scarcely had he begun when a sharp attack of lumbago fell upon him; for two or three days it was torture to support himself at the desk, and he moved about like a cripple. Upon this ensued headaches, sore throat, general enfeeblement. And before the end of the fortnight it was necessary to think of raising another small sum of money; he took his watch to the pawnbroker's (you can imagine that it would not stand as security for much), and sold a few more books. All this notwithstanding, here was the novel at length finished. When he had written 'The End' he lay back, closed his eyes, and let time pass in blankness for a quarter of an hour.

"It remained to determine the title. But his brain refused another effort; after a few minutes' feeble search he simply took the name of the chief female character, Margaret Home. That must do for the book. Already, with the penning of the last word, all its scenes, personages, dialogues had slipped away into oblivion; he knew and cared nothing more about them."   GEORGE GISSING, *New Grub Street*